RUDOLF STEINER (1861–1925) called his spiritual philosophy 'anthroposophy', meaning 'wisdom of the human being'. As a highly developed seer, he based his work on direct knowledge and perception of spiritual dimensions. He initiated a modern and universal 'science of spirit', accessible to anyone willing to exercise clear and unprejudiced thinking.

From his spiritual investigations Steiner provided suggestions for the renewal of many activities, including education (both general and special), agriculture, medicine, economics, architecture, science, philosophy, religion and the arts. Today there are thousands of schools, clinics, farms and other organizations involved in practical work based on his principles. His many published works feature his research into the spiritual nature of the human being, the evolution of the world and humanity, and methods of personal development. Steiner wrote some 30 books and delivered over 6,000 lectures across Europe. In 1924 he founded the General Anthroposophical Society, which today has branches throughout the world.

EURYTHMY

Practical Applications

Also in this series:

(Practical Applications)
Agriculture
Architecture
Art
Education
Medicine
Religion
Science
Social and Political Science

(Esoteric)
Alchemy
Atlantis
Christian Rozenkreutz
The Druids
The Goddess
The Holy Grail

RUDOLF STEINER

EURYTHMY

An Introductory Reader

*Compiled with an introduction,
commentary and notes by
Beth Usher*

Sophia Books

All translations revised by Christian von Arnim

Sophia Books
An imprint of Rudolf Steiner Press
Hillside House, The Square
Forest Row, RH18 5ES

www.rudolfsteinerpress.com

Published by Rudolf Steiner Press 2006

For earlier English publications of individual selections please
see pp. 299–306

The material by Rudolf Steiner was originally published in
German in various volumes of the 'GA' (*Rudolf Steiner
Gesamtausgabe* or Collected Works) by Rudolf Steiner Verlag,
Dornach (for further information see pp. 299–306). This
authorized volume is published by permission of the Rudolf
Steiner Nachlassverwaltung, Dornach

A catalogue record for this book is available from the British
Library

ISBN-10: 1 85584 114 2
ISBN-13: 978 185584 114 7

Cover photo by Charlotte Fischer, courtesy Eurythmeum
Stuttgart/Goetheanum-Bühne Dornach
Cover design by Andrew Morgan
Typeset in Great Britain by DP Photosetting
Printed by Cromwell Press Ltd., Trowbridge, Wilts.

Contents

List of Illustrations

Introduction

by Beth Usher

Eurythmy is a new art of movement, which developed out of Rudolf Steiner's creative insights in the early 1900s. Though nearly a hundred years old, the art itself is still being born into new languages, new geographical regions, new life situations. The original lessons from Rudolf Steiner have not yet revealed their full scope even after lifetimes of work. One can compare this growth with the evolution of the musical fugue. Composers had been writing fugues for two hundred years before Johann Sebastian Bach created the crown with his *Art of Fugue*. Conscious development evolves slowly through time.

The early 1900s saw an explosion of new impulses in the art world throughout Europe, Russia and the Americas. Architecture, sculpture, painting, music, dance, drama, poetry — all broke through the old forms, creating new laws or no laws in attempts to express the soul of modern times. The century that saw these artistic explosions also was scarred by some of the greatest social catastrophes in human history. The early 2000s are seeing an art world encompassing brilliant achievements, including *avant garde* music performed with the sound of furniture movements in the score, brush painting with light, dancing to poetry read through a reducer, performance art wrapping the artist in a boa constrictor on ice, chamber music interspersed with measures of the spoken word, digital electronic media in all forms laced into drama, fabric art with synthetic material never seen before. Eurythmy has entered onto this stage.

Rudolf Steiner said repeatedly that eurythmy would one day take its place beside the older arts. Where in this context, one may ask, is eurythmy's place?

Eurythmy did not grow out of modern dance. It grew from the artistic impulse which Rudolf Steiner gave at the Theosophical Congress in Munich in 1907. Never before had an esoteric school given artistic expression to the content of spiritual teaching. When the first eurythmy lessons began in 1912, works of the visual arts, speech, architecture, music, poetry and drama had already begun to appear out of the stream of anthroposophy. As the eurythmy work developed, Rudolf Steiner invited eurythmists to his lectures. We can see now how he wove the content of his spiritual teaching into the eurythmy forms, gestures and indications. *The Gospel of St Mark*, the *Four Mystery Dramas*, *Wonders of the World*, *Genesis*, *The Fifth Gospel*, and *Occult Reading and Hearing* were some of the lecture courses given while the first eurythmists were learning to walk.

We read in the lecture excerpt in Part One, 'Impulses of transformation for the human being's artistic evolution', that eurythmy contains the laws of our 'Life Spirit', a higher element of the human being. Life Spirit, or Buddhi, refers to a level of perfection we will only reach in the very distant future. Rudolf Steiner considered all eurythmy done in his time to be the most elementary beginning because of the nature of Life Spirit, which is present in the environment of soul and spirit, but still outside the human being. Eurythmy is an art of the future.

Eurythmy is an art of the sun. This statement is not contained in the literature, but it is this writer's view that Rudolf Steiner intentionally juxtaposed the deepest esoteric lectures about the sun with the continually evolving work in eurythmy. 'A Lecture on Eurythmy' was given in the context of the *Evolution of Consciousness* summer course at Penmaenmawr, North Wales. The evening before, he had spoken about 'The Interplay of Various Worlds': 'When anyone learns to master consciously the hidden Sun forces, so that he does not use the outspread darkness for seeing reflected images but carries into the darkness the inner light kindled in soul and spirit through meditation and concentration; when he becomes able to fill with inner soul forces the space otherwise lit up by the physical sun so that he can illuminate it with the light of his own soul and spirit, then indeed conscious Imagination arises.'

The indications from the Light Course, reproduced in Part Two, were given simultaneously with *The Genius of Language* lectures, both courses for teachers. A study of light, gift from the sun, is woven with a study of the word at Christmastime, 1919. Eurythmy is mentioned in the language lectures. Very quickly, the words '*Die Sonne* [sun] *das Gold, diesen Tag* [gold, on this day]' follow as examples on the subsequent pages. The 'Birth of the Light' permeates the teacher training.

A picture of the threefold sun precedes the discussion of the zodiac in the quote from *Cosmosophy*, Vol. II, found in Part Three. 'At all times, even when people had only instinctive knowledge, it was said that the sun was threefold in character, the source of light, life and love. This trinity is to be found in the sun... The life of this sun produces light in the outside world, love in our hearts, and life in our dealings with the outside world. Its location is midway between the life of breathing and the life of the circulation, as the ancients also knew. Between those two lives lies the heart, which does not act as a motor but reflects the interplay between circulation and breathing.' The lecture continues with a discussion of the movements of the zodiac in relation to our internal organs, and how eurythmy is the direct image of the relationship human beings have to the cosmos.

In the excerpts on stage lighting in Part Four, the light, which is of the soul, is artistically expressed through the lightening of the stage picture. This does not mean one should be speaking about the sun breaking through the clouds when the stage lights become brighter. The lighting is given over to movement, a kind of light eurythmy. The eurythmist and light eurythmy together produce a lightening, the activity of the sun. Such a quality can occur in many forms of music and speech. One example of Rudolf Steiner's numerous and wondrously varied indications for stage lighting is given in this chapter.

The final selection in this book shows the programme for the first eurythmy performance of the Foundation Stone Meditation. This verse had been 'laid in the hearts of the members' of the Anthroposophical Society at the Christmas Conference (December 1923) several months before. Rudolf Steiner spoke of the Mysteries of the Sun four months after the conference during the Easter festival, April 1924. The verse was performed in eurythmy for the first time at this Easter festival. The introduction to a eurythmy performance, entitled 'Movement: the speech of the soul', in Part One of this book, was also part of the Easter festival. The last stanza of the Foundation Stone, a powerful meditative verse in four parts, speaks of light in many forms, 'O Light Divine, O Sun of Christ'. Christ, as Rudolf Steiner speaks of him, is the incarnation of the Word, wisdom, love itself, a 'Supreme Being who has so purified his astral body or Kama that it has been changed into Buddhi'. (The advanced student of anthroposophy will recognize this as a transformation on a higher level than in a normal human life.) This refers us back to the beginning of the book, 'Impulses of Transformation', where eurythmy is described as the art proceeding from Buddhi. We may also refer to the Speech Eurythmy Course, 'Eurythmic technique must be won out of a love for eurythmy, for in truth, everything must proceed out of love.' The reader is free to draw his own conclusions on the thesis that we have in eurythmy the gift of an art of the sun.

Rudolf Steiner (1861–1925) was an Austrian philosopher, who has been counted among history's 'Great Initiates' by Edouard Schuré in the book of that title. His insights transforming education, social thought, medicine, agriculture, philosophy and the arts have spread from a few indications to activities spanning the globe. In the midst of all his other work, he made eurythmy a priority.

He toured Europe with the first eurythmists when public performances were finally possible. The first seven years, from 1912 to 1919, were a time of intensive training and creative collaboration. Two full courses as well as indications for eurythmy within dramatic scenes from J.W. v. Goethe's *Faust* gave the eurythmists a wealth of material to rehearse. Many wonderful memoirs of the first eurythmist, Lory Smits, and others, who developed the art in those early years, have been published in English. Later courses in eurythmy therapy, tone and speech eurythmy did not exhaust the scope Rudolf Steiner had intended. He spoke of his intention to give two more full eurythmy courses; and throughout, he spoke of this as a beginning.

Marie Steiner, Rudolf Steiner's wife and co-worker, laboured with ceaseless fire to develop eurythmy as well as an art of speech arising out of anthroposophy, which so essentially completes speech eurythmy. She says of the 1924 Speech Eurythmy Course: 'We united for this course as if for a united festival ... the entire course had the character of an immediate fresh improvisation. Drawings were quickly made on the blackboard; exercises for exemplification were carried out by the young women; everything came about in the form of conversation and collaboration, not in mere lecturing. This was often the character of instruction given by Rudolf Steiner to his students, but never in such high degree as in this course on eurythmy.' Juliet Compton-Burnett was an English eurythmy teacher who participated in the 1924 Speech Eurythmy Course. She describes her experience: 'Anticipation had run high, but who could have foreseen the reality? Cosmic horizons widened, and the eurythmists were carried on the wings of his spirit into undreamed of realms, and were strengthened in their resolves when he spoke of his love for this new art which he had given to the world.' Indeed, Marie Steiner observed, 'eurythmy was one of the most beloved spiritual children of Rudolf Steiner'.

In addition to the five courses and several hundred introductions to performances, he drew eurythmy choreography, 1300 forms for poems in several languages and for musical selections with a variety of musical instruments. One example of a standard form and one sketch have been included in Part Four on eurythmy as a performing art. Eurythmists have since learned to create simpler forms for stage eurythmy and classroom use. In the beginning years, however, Rudolf Steiner drew all the forms that the eurythmists performed. In a memoir from his personal secretary, Günther Wachsmuth, we read, 'Many of these forms he drew during rehearsals with chalk upon the floor of the stage, most of them, however, on a sheet of paper. Many of these sketches and drawings for the forms of eurythmy have been preserved from the earliest years and are still rendering service to artists both for purposes of teaching and also for actual programmes.' The forms are, in themselves, teachers.

Juliet Compton-Burnett pointed to the spiritual integrity of these forms when she characterized the strictness and pliancy of Rudolf Steiner's approach: 'A certain eurythmist was showing a poem by Albert Steffen. As she finished, Rudolf Steiner got up and said, "That will not do"; and he went on to say that for this poem he had already given a form and this being so, no other form should be used. "For any poem there is only one true form" — his voice, stern and earnest, remains in my memory. What might have appeared a slight matter was once and for all given its full significance.' She said, in contrast, on another occasion, he quickly changed a costume indication to accommodate the arrangement of a programme.

Eurythmy has grown into the three professions to which Rudolf Steiner refers in his many introductions to performances. As a stage art, it has soared as symphonies and operas, sagas and sonnets. The practice of eurythmy in Waldorf schools with children of all ages has spread worldwide. High school students are enthusiastically forming their own performing groups, touring even internationally. An extension of teaching adult courses has brought eurythmy into the workplace, helping working people at all levels to see each other and the challenges of their daily tasks in a new light. Eurythmy therapy has expanded into anthroposophical hospitals and clinics, with specialties developing in ophthalmology, cardiology, dentistry, psychiatry, oncology and internal medicine. Though thousands of people have experienced eurythmy through one of these professions since its inception, the art remains virtually unknown to the general population.

This volume may encourage the reader to pursue a spark of interest in what eurythmy can bring to humanity. Further reading might include exploring the history of eurythmy, as well as the fuller context of the many excerpts and individual lectures included here. Of course, doing or seeing eurythmy once or even daily over the course of decades is the best way to come to understand what is meant here.

1. In the beginning, God created out of movement

Rudolf Steiner strove to convey that everyone on earth now has the potential to directly perceive spiritual activity. Such perception can resurrect creative powers for artistic work. The art of eurythmy, when filled with such spiritual activity, so moves the human soul that it gives proof of our real participation in the supersensory world. The 'Supersensory origin of the arts' lecture excerpt develops this thought.

One of the most essential principles of eurythmy comes in the 'About the nature of gestures' lecture. The poet, the artist, must bring the heart to speak. The heart does not live in the physical sounds; the heart lives in the inner relationship of the sounds. The movement is a sound stream, the flow of a river of sound. Eurythmy makes this inaudible heart stream visible.

We read in Eurythmy as Visible Speech *that God makes eurythmy movements, and out of his eurythmy rises the form of the human being. We are created out of sound.*

Must I remain unable to speak?

An anthroposophical book is meant to be received into inner experience. This leads to the gradual awakening of a certain understanding. It may be a very faint, inner experience. But it can—indeed, should—occur. And the greater depth gained through the exercises described in *How to Know Higher Worlds*[1] is just that—a fortifying deepening. This is necessary for progress on the spiritual path; but a properly written anthroposophical book should awaken the spiritual life of the reader, and not merely be a collection of information. Reading it should be more than reading; it should be an experience accompanied by inner shocks, tensions and resolutions.

I realize how far the substance and inner power of my books are from always invoking such an experience in the soul of the reader. But I also know that my inner struggle over every page was to attain as much as possible in this way. I do not adopt a style that allows subjective feelings to be detected in the sentences. In writing, I subdue what comes from warmth and deeper feelings to a dry, mathematical style. This style alone can be an awakener, for the readers themselves must awaken inner warmth and feeling. They cannot let those feelings simply flow into them from a description while their attentiveness remains passive.

Artistic interests were barely cultivated at all within the Theosophical Society.[2] From a certain perspective, this was completely understandable, but this had to change before a proper spiritual attitude could thrive. Members of such a society tend to focus all their interests primarily on the reality of spiritual life. In the sensory world, the human being appears to them as merely a transitory existence, severed from spirit. Artistic activity seems to exist within that severed existence. Thus, it seems to be outside of the spiritual reality that is sought. Because of this, artists did not feel at home in the Theosophical Society.

It was important to Marie von Sivers[3] and to me that the arts should come to life within the society. Consequently, spirit knowledge indeed takes in the whole of human existence. All of the soul forces are stimulated. The light from inner, spiritual experience shines into the creating imagination.

But here something enters that creates hindrances. Artists have some anxiety about their imagination being illumined by the world of spirit. They prefer to remain unaware of the exercise of the soul world. And this feeling is appropriate when it is a matter of the imagination being 'stimulated' by the conscious thought element that has dominated culture since the beginning of the era of the consciousness soul. This 'stimulation' through human intellectuality has a deadening effect on art.

Just the opposite occurs, however, when directly perceived spiritual meaning fills the imagination with light. All the creative powers that have ever led to art among humanity are resurrected in this way. Marie von Sivers was truly accomplished in the art of speech formation and greatly gifted in dramatic art. A sphere of art was thus present within the anthroposophical activity, and based on this we could test the fertility of spiritual perception for art.

The evolution of the consciousness soul exposes the

'word' to danger from two directions. Speech serves as mediator in society and it communicates logical, intellectual knowledge. In both directions the word loses its inherent value. It must adapt to the meaning of what it is intended to express. It must allow ignorance of the fact that the sound, tone and formation of tone itself contain a reality. The beauty—the shining of the vowel and the character of the consonant—is lost in speech. The vowel loses its soul and the consonant becomes void of spirit. Speech entirely vacates the realm from which it originates—spirit. It becomes the servant of intellectual knowledge and serves a society that flees spirit. It is torn completely from the realm of art.[4]

True spiritual perception enters the 'experience of word' as if by instinct. It learns to feel its way into the vowel's reverberation sustained by the soul and into the consonant's painting energized by spirit. Gradually it begins to understand the mysterious evolution of speech, the mystery that at one time divine spiritual beings were able to speak to the human soul through the word, whereas now it is merely a means of communication in the physical world.

One needs enthusiasm kindled by this spiritual insight to lead the word back to its own sphere. Marie von Sivers developed such enthusiasm. Thus she brought to the anthroposophical movement the possibility of artistically cultivating speech and speech formation. In this way, the cultivation of recitation and declamation as an art was added to the activity of communicating spiritual knowledge, and this played an increasing role in anthroposophical events.

Marie von Sivers's recitations at those events were the beginning of the impact of art on the anthroposophical movement. The dramatic performances that later took place in Munich along with the anthroposophical courses developed directly from those recitations (initially given to supplement the lectures).[5]

Because we could develop art through spiritual knowledge, we increasingly penetrated the truth of modern spiritual experience. Art originally grew out of dreamy, pictorial experiences of spirit. As this spirit experience receded in the course of human evolution, art had to find its way alone.[6] It must find its way again to a unity with spiritual experience when, in new form, this experience becomes part of human cultural development.

The supersensory origin of the arts

If we have a narrow-minded view of the arts we create during life and see them as being connected only to the period between birth and death, we actually deprive artistic creativity of all meaning. For artistic creativity most certainly means carrying supersensory spiritual worlds into the physical world of the senses. We bring architecture, sculpture, painting, music and poetry into the world of physical experience simply because we feel the pressure of what we carry within us from pre-earthly existence, because when awake we feel the pressure of what we carry within us as a result of our spiritual life during sleep, and because we feel the pressure of something already in us that will shape us after death. That people usually do not speak about supersensory worlds simply stems from the fact that they do not understand the world of the senses either. And above all, they do not understand something that was once known to the spiritual culture of humanity before it was lost and became an external phenomenon, namely, art.

If we learn to understand art, it becomes a real proof of human immortality and of life before birth. This is what we need in order to expand our consciousness beyond the horizon of birth and death, so that we can link what we have during life on the physical earth to the life that transcends the physical plane.

If we work creatively out of such knowledge as the spiritual science of anthroposophy, which aims to understand the spiritual world and to receive it into our ideas and thoughts, into our feelings, perceptions and will, it will prepare the ground for an art that synthesizes in some way what precedes birth and what follows death.

Let's consider the art of eurythmy, where we set the human body itself in motion. What exactly are we setting in motion? We are setting the human organism in motion; we are making its limbs move. The limbs, more than any other part of the human body, are what pass over into the life of the next incarnation. They point to the future, to what comes after death. But how do we shape the limb movements we bring forth in eurythmy? In the sense realm and in the supersensory realm we study how the larynx and all the speech organs have been brought over from the previous life and shaped by the intellectual potentials of the head and the feeling potentials of the chest. We directly link what precedes birth with what follows death. In a certain sense, we take from earthly life only the physical medium, the actual human being who is the tool or instrument for eurythmy. But we allow this human being to make manifest what we study inwardly, what is already prepared in us as a result of previous lives; we transfer this to our limbs, which are the part of us where life after death is being shaped in advance. Eurythmy shapes and moves the human organism in a way that furnishes direct external proof of our participation in the supersensory world. In having people do eurythmy, we link them directly to the supersensory world.

Wherever art is developed on the basis of a truly artistic attitude, it bears witness to our connection to the supersensory worlds. And if in our time we human beings are called upon to take the gods into our own soul forces, as it were, so that we no longer wait in pious faith for the gods to give us one thing or another, but try instead to take action as though the gods were living in our active will, then the time has indeed come, if humankind will only experience it, when we must take the step from external, objectively formed arts, as it were, to an art form that will assume quite different dimensions and forms in the future, an art form that portrays the supersensory world directly. How could it be otherwise? Spiritual science itself wants to present the supersensory directly, so it is bound to use its resources to create an art of this kind.

As for its educational applications, people who are educated along these lines will gradually come to find it quite natural to believe that they are supersensory beings, because they move their hands, arms and legs in such a way that the forces of the supersensory world are active in them. It is the soul of the human being, the supersensory soul, that begins to move in eurythmy. It is the living expression of the supersensory that comes to light in eurythmy movements.

Everything spiritual science brings us is really in inner harmony with itself. On the one hand, it brings us these things so that we may more deeply and intensely comprehend the life we are engaged in, so that we may learn to turn our gaze to the living proof of the reality of existence before birth and after death. On the other hand, it introduces our supersensory element into our will.

This is the inner cohesiveness underlying an anthroposophically oriented spiritual-scientific striving. This is how spiritual science will expand human consciousness. It will no longer be possible for people to make their way through the world as they have been doing in the age of materialism, when they have been able to survey only what takes place between birth and death. Although they may also believe in something else that promises bliss and redemption, they can form no concept of this 'something else'. They can only listen to sentimental sermons about it;

in actuality it is empty of content. Through spiritual science, human beings are meant to receive real content from the spiritual world once again. We are meant to be released from the life of abstraction, from the life that refuses to go beyond the perceptions and thoughts that lie between birth and death, from a life that at most takes in some indefinite verbal indications of the spiritual world. Spiritual science will infuse us with a consciousness that will widen our horizon and enable us to be aware of the supersensory world even as we live and work in the physical world.

It is true enough that we go through the world today knowing at, say, the age of 30 that the foundation for what we are now was laid in us when we were 10 or 15. This much we can remember. If we read something at age 30, we remember that the present moment is linked to the time 22 or 23 years ago when we were learning to read. But what we do not notice is that between birth and death we constantly have pulsing within us the experiences we underwent between our last death and our present birth. Let's look at what has been born out of these forces in architecture and in sculpture. If we understand this correctly, we will also be able to apply it to our lives in the right way and to achieve once again a sense of how prose is fashioned into the rhythm, metre, alliteration and assonance of poetry, even though this may be considered superfluous to ordinary prosaic life. Then we will form the right link between this special nuance of feeling and the immortal kernel of our being which we carry with us through death. We will say that it would be impossible for anyone to become a poet unless all human beings possessed the actual creative element of the poet, namely the force that already resides within us but does not become outwardly alive until after death.[7]

This draws the supersensory into our ordinary consciousness, which must expand again if humanity does not intend to sink further into the depths we have plunged into as a result of a contracted consciousness that makes us live only in what happens between birth and death, allowing us at most to hear preaching about what is present in the supersensory world.

You see, we encounter spiritual science everywhere, whenever we speak about the most important cultural needs of our time.

Impulses of transformation for the human being's artistic evolution

In the course of the following considerations, I shall be speaking to you about the important impulses of transformation present in our era for the artistic evolution of humankind. I would like to connect this with what may occur to you as a result of your own observation of this building (the Goetheanum), or rather with that of which this building is merely a beginning. But as a basis for these considerations it will be necessary to establish a connection between art and the knowledge we have gained about the human being and his relationship with the world in general. I will begin today with these seemingly more theoretical considerations and continue tomorrow with our actual theme concerning the impulses of transformation in artistic development.

Though I said that I would begin today with a seemingly more theoretical basis, in actual fact anyone who looks upon spiritual science as something living will find these preliminaries very much alive and not at all theoretical. They will, however, only be quite clear to those for whom the ideas of physical body, etheric body, astral body, ego, and so on, are not mere designations in a diagram of the human being's being but the expression of actual experiences in feelings and ideas relating to the spiritual world.

If we consider the different forms of art, it appears that architecture is the one that has become most separated from the human being as a whole. Architecture is separated from the human being because it is placed at the service of our external impulses, either those of utility, which call for utilitarian structures, or those having idealistic aims, as in the case of religious buildings. We shall see during the course of the lecture how other forms of art have a more intimate connection with the real being of the human being than has architecture. Architecture is in some way detached from what we describe as the laws of the human being's inner being. And yet, seen from the point of view of spiritual science, this external character of architecture very largely disappears.

When we begin to look at the human being, the part that first strikes us, because it is the most outward, is the physical body. But this physical body is permeated and penetrated and filled by the etheric body. The physical body might simply be called a spatial body or described as being organized in space. But the etheric body, which dwells in the physical body and, as you know, also extends beyond the limits of the physical body and is intimately connected with the whole cosmos, cannot be contemplated without the aid of time. Basically everything in the etheric body is rhythm, a cyclical rhythm of movement or activity, and it has a spatial character only in as far as it inhabits the physical body. For human imaginative perception, it is true, the etheric body also has to be conceived in spatial pictures, but these do not show its essential nature, which is cyclic, rhythmical, moving in time.

Music takes up no space but is solely present in time. In the same way, what matters with regard to the human etheric body in reality (not in the imaginative picture we draw) is mobility, movement, formative activity in rhythmic or musical sequence, in fact the quality of time. Of course, this is a difficult thing for the human mind to conceive, accustomed as it is to relating everything to space; but in order to gain a clear concept of the etheric body we must try much harder to allow musical ideas rather than spatial ideas to come to our aid.

In order to bring to the fore another characteristic of the etheric body it can be said that, occupying the physical body and extending, as it does, its activity and rhythmical play into this physical body, it is above all a body of forces. It is a flowing-out of forces, a manifestation of forces, and we notice them in a number of phenomena that occur during the course of a person's life. One of these phenomena, to which not much attention is paid by external science or from an outward view of the world, but one which we have often stressed, is the ability of the human being to stand upright. On entering the world at birth we are not yet able to assume this vertical posture, which is the most important of all postures for the human being. We have to acquire the ability. It is true that this is initiated by the astral body, which as it were transfers its power of upward extension to the etheric body, but it is the latter which in the course of time sets about raising the physical body into a vertical position. Here we see the living interplay of the astral and etheric bodies in the formation of the physical body.

But this acquisition of the upright posture is only the most striking of these phenomena. Whenever we lift a hand a similar process takes place. In our ego we can only hold the thought of lifting a hand; this thought must immediately act upon the astral body, and the astral body transfers its activity, which lives in it as an impulse, to the etheric body. And what happens then? Let us assume that someone is holding his hand in a horizontal position. Now he forms the idea: I want to raise my hand a little bit higher. The idea, which in life is followed by the act of lifting the hand, passes over to the astral body; there an impulse arises and passes over from the astral body to the etheric body. And now the following happens in the etheric body: the hand is horizontal to begin with; then the etheric body is drawn up higher, followed by the movement of the physical hand after what occurs first as a development of force in the etheric body. The physical hand follows the etheric.[8]

I shall explain the whole process tomorrow. At the moment I simply want to point out that making any movement involves a development of force which is followed by a state of equilibrium. In the life of our organism we are continually dealing with a development of force followed by a state of equilibrium. Of course the human being has no conscious knowledge of what is really going on within him; but what takes place is so infinitely wise that the cleverness of the human ego is nothing by comparison. We would be unable to move a hand if we had to depend on our own cleverness and knowledge alone; for the subtle forces developed by the astral body in the etheric body and then passed on to the physical body are quite inaccessible to ordinary human knowledge. And the wisdom developed in this process is millions of times greater than that required by a watchmaker in making a watch.

We do not usually think of this, but such wisdom actually has to be developed. It must be developed and it is developed as a result of our being left to ourselves with our ego. But the moment the ego sends the impulses of its idea into the astral body we need the help of another being; unaided we can do nothing here. We are dependent on help from a being belonging to the hierarchy of the angels. For even the tiniest movement of a finger we need the assistance of a being whose wisdom is far in advance of our own. We could do nothing but lie on the earth immobile, having ideas in utter rigidity, if the beings of the higher hierarchies did not constantly surround us with their activity.

Therefore the first step towards initiation[9] is to gain an understanding of how these forces act upon the human being.

I have tried to show here what is involved even in a movement as simple as resting the head in the hand. We learn to know, in the form of a spatial system of lines and forces, the outside of our being, what happens to our physical body through the activity of the etheric body. If we carry this spatial system of lines and forces that is constantly active in us out into the world, and if we organize matter according to this system, then architecture arises. All architecture consists in separating from ourselves this system of forces and placing it outside in space. Thus we may say: here we have the outer boundary of our physical body, and if we push the inner organization, which has been impressed by the etheric body onto the physical body, outside this boundary, then architecture arises. All the laws present in the architectural utilization of matter are found also in the human body. When we project the specific organization of the human body into the space outside it, then we have architecture.

Now we know, in our way of looking at things, that the etheric body is attached to the physical body. Looking once more at any work of architecture, what can we say about it? We can say that here, carried into the space outside us, is the interaction between vertical and horizontal and between forces that react together, all of which are otherwise to be found within the human physical body.

In the same way we can convey what streams from the etheric body into the physical body not outside ourselves this time, but down from the etheric into the physical body. In other words we can bring about something which we do not separate from ourselves by placing it outside us, but which we only push down into ourselves. This is the process by which the laws of the etheric body, which it has received from the astral body, can become physical, just as in architecture the laws of the physical body are projected into the space outside us. Through this process, sculpture arises out of the etheric body, just as architecture arises out of the physical body. In a way we push the laws of the etheric body down one step.

Physical body

                              Architecture

Etheric body

                              Sculpture

Just as in architecture we push the laws of the physical body into the space outside us, so in sculpture we push the laws of the etheric body one step downwards. We do not separate these laws from ourselves, we push them directly into our own form. Just as we find in architecture the expression of the laws of our own physical body, so we find in sculpture the natural laws of our etheric body; we simply transfer this inner order into our works of sculpture. In architecture we transplant into the space outside ourselves nothing but the laws of the physical body, its spatial lines and interplay of forces, taking nothing of the etheric body, nothing of the astral body, nothing of the ego. In the same way, where sculpture is concerned, we take only the laws of the etheric body and bring them down one step lower, using nothing of the astral body and nothing of the ego except in so far as they send impulses into the etheric body. This is why a work of sculpture appears to be alive. It would actually be alive if it contained also the ego and the astral body. So if we seek the laws of sculpture we must realize that they are in fact the laws of our etheric body, just as the laws of architecture are to be seen in the laws of our physical body.

If we do the same in connection with the astral body, pushing what is in us of an astral nature a step lower down into the etheric body, we are pushing down what lives inwardly in the human being. Now there is nothing that could truly have a spatial nature, for the astral body, when it moves down into the etheric body, is not entering a spatial element—the etheric body is rhythmic and harmonious, not spatial. Therefore the result can only be a picture, indeed a real picture—in fact, the art of painting. Painting is the form of art that contains the laws of our astral body, just as sculpture contains the laws of our etheric body and architecture those of our physical body.

Physical body

                                    Architecture

Etheric body

                                    Sculpture

Astral body

                                    Painting

If we now take the fourth member of the human being, the ego, and push it with its laws down into the astral body, there allowing it to move and act, then we obtain yet another form of art. This art does not contain what works in the ego as something which can be expressed in language or ordinary ideas; it is something that has moved from the ego down one step towards the subconscious. It is as though the horizon of consciousness were to be moved down by the amount of half an element of the human being. We take half a step downward, our ego descends into the astral body: music is born.

Physical Body

                                    Architecture

Etheric Body

                                    Sculpture

Astral Body

                                    Painting

Ego

                                    Music

So music contains the laws of our ego, though not as they are manifested in ordinary, everyday life but pressed down into the subconscious, into the astral body. The ego dives, as it were, beneath the surface of the astral body, there to flow and stream within the organization of the astral body.

If we go on to speak about the higher members of the human being, starting with the Spirit Self, we can refer to them only as something which is still outside the human being. For in this fifth post-Atlantean epoch[10] we are only just beginning to make this Spirit Self one of our inner elements. But if we accept it as a gift from a higher sphere and lower it into our ego, if we dive down, like a swimmer into the water, into our ego, taking with us what as yet can only be dimly felt of the Spirit Self, then poetry is born.

Physical Body	
	Architecture
Etheric Body	
	Sculpture
Astral Body	
	Painting
Ego	
	Music
Spirit Self	
	Poetry

And proceeding still further, one can say, though to a limited extent: round about us, in the environment of soul and spirit, which we shall absorb at a later stage, the Life

Spirit is also present. Therefore one day the Life Spirit may come to be lowered into the Spirit Self. But of course at the moment this is something that will only reach a certain degree of perfection in the very distant future. For when he tries to lower the Life Spirit into the Spirit Self, the human being will have to be living entirely in an element which as yet is absolutely strange to him. So what we can say in this domain is like the babbling of a child when compared with the later perfection of speech. One can foresee for the far distant future that there will be an art of great perfection that will stand out beyond poetry, as poetry stands out beyond music, music beyond painting, painting beyond sculpture, and sculpture beyond architecture (this being a question not of superiority, but of arrangement). You will guess, of course, that I am referring to something of which we know only the most elementary beginnings today, something of which we can only receive the very first indications: the art of eurythmy.

Eurythmy is indeed something that must appear in human evolution at this time, but there is no call for pride, for at present it can be a mere babbling compared with what it will become in the future.

Physical Body

　　　　　　　　　　　　Architecture

Etheric Body

　　　　　　　　　　　　Sculpture

Astral Body

　　　　　　　　　　　　Painting

Ego

                          Music

Spirit Self

                          Poetry

Life Spirit

                          Eurythmy

We can now begin at any point with a somewhat more extended view. But in order to do so we must realize that the organization of the human being is not nearly as simple as we would like to imagine in our intellectual indolence.

It is incredibly easy simply to imagine that the human being consists of physical body, etheric body, astral body, ego, and so on. If one is able to enumerate these various elements and has an approximate conception of them, one may easily consider this rather simple form of knowledge quite satisfactory. But things are not so simple. Physical body, etheric body, astral body, ego are not simply sheaths which fit easily into one another; they are, on the contrary, very complex structures. Take, for instance, the astral body. It is not enough merely to say this is the astral body and leave it at that. Things are much more complicated.

Words here are only an approximation, but we could say that the astral body, for instance, is in itself structured and consists of seven elements. Just as the human being can be said to have seven elements (physical body, etheric body, astral body, ego, Spirit Self, Life Spirit, Spirit Man), so the astral body has a connection with each of these.

There is a 'thinnest' part of the astral body which could be described as being especially moulded and fashioned for the physical body. That is to say there is a living system of laws in the astral body for the physical body, a living system of laws in the astral body for the etheric body, a living system of laws in the astral body for itself, a living system of laws in the astral body for the ego, a living system of laws in the astral body for the Spirit Self, for the Life Spirit, and for Spirit Man. Thus each element of the human being has in turn seven elements. So taking into consideration that the human being consists of seven elements which are in turn each structured into seven elements, we already find we have a total of 49 elements. This of course sounds perfectly horrible to modern psychologists who like to regard the soul as a unity and would prefer to have nothing to do with these things. But for true knowledge, which must gradually arise in the course of the spiritual evolution of mankind, it is certainly not without significance. For when we know that the astral body is sevenfold in its nature and that it is an organism of inner living impulses, then we shall say to ourselves: within this astral body, with its sevenfold organization, individual activities must surely take place between the various elements. The part of the astral body that corresponds to the physical body must have a certain interplay with the part that corresponds to the etheric body and with the part that corresponds to the astral body itself, and so on. These are no mere abstract suppositions; it is quite possible in the human organism for a person to feel inwardly—though more subconsciously than consciously—a movement of that part of the astral body which corresponds to the physical body. And then something may produce another movement which will have to start in that element of the astral body that corresponds to the astral body itself, and so on. This is not mere theory; it really happens.

Now imagine the seven members of the astral body to be interrelated as are the tones of the scale: tonic, second, third, fourth, etc. If you allow the effect of a melody to work upon you, you will find that your human organization permits this to occur because the various tones of the melody are experienced inwardly in the corresponding elements of the astral body. The interval of a third is experienced in the part of the astral body that corresponds to the astral body itself. A fourth is experienced in the part of the astral body that—well, let us now be more specific—corresponds to the intellectual or mind soul. A fifth is experienced in the part of the astral body that corresponds to the consciousness or spiritual soul. And remembering that when we divide the human organism more exactly we find it contains nine elements, we must, accordingly, structure the astral body in the same way. Instead of referring to 'the element of the astral body that corresponds to the physical body' when enumerating the various elements, I could now say 'the element experienced in the tonic'. Instead of 'the element of the astral body that corresponds to the etheric body', I could say 'the element experienced in the second'. And instead of saying 'the element of the astral body that corresponds to the astral body itself' I could say 'the element experienced in the third'.

	—		
	—		
	—		
Fifth	—	Consciousness soul	
Fourth	—	Intellectual soul	
			Sentient soul
Third	—	Astral body	<
			Astral body
Second	—	Etheric body	
Tonic	—	Physical body	

You can now also see that the existence of the major third and the minor third really corresponds to the incorporation of the astral body in our whole human organization. If you look up the relevant passage in my book *Theosophy*, you will see that there is an overlap of the astral body with what we call the sentient soul. Therefore what I described as an interval of a third can correspond either to the astral body or to the sentient soul: in the one case we have the major third and in the other the minor third.

It is a fact that our ability to experience a musical work of art depends upon this inner musical activity of the astral body. However, while we listen to the music with our ego we immediately submerge the experience into our astral body, into certain realms which are subconscious.

This leads us to a very important fact. Let us look at ourselves as astral beings, as possessors of an astral body. What is our nature in this respect? As astral beings we have been created out of the cosmos according to musical laws. Inasmuch as we are astral beings we are musically connected with the cosmos. We are ourselves an instrument. Let us now suppose that we do not need to hear the physical sound of tones, but are able to listen to the creative activity that has brought us into existence as astral beings out of the cosmos. In such a state we would hear the universal music, what has always been called the music of the spheres. Let us suppose that we are able to dive down consciously into our astral entity, developing its spiritual strength to such an extent that we can hear the creative activity of the cosmic music; we could then say: with the help of our astral body the cosmos is playing our own being. This thought, which I have just expressed to you, was alive in human beings in ancient times, really alive. And in pointing this out we are also pointing to the way in which right into the fifth post-Atlantean epoch human evolution has become more and more materialistic. For we all know that this thought is not alive in the external human culture of today; humanity knows nothing about the fact that, so far as the astral body is concerned, the human being is a musical instrument.

But this was not always the case, and the fact that it was not always the case has been forgotten. For there was a time when people said: a man once lived who was called John, and this John was able to transport himself into a state of spiritual awareness in which he could hear the music of the heavenly Jerusalem. They said all earthly music can only be a copy of the heavenly music which began with the creation of humankind. And the more religious part of humanity felt that by passing over into the world of physical desires human beings had absorbed impulses which veiled and darkened the celestial music for them. But at the same time they felt that there must exist in human evolution — through purification from the external chaos of life — a road leading to the goal of hearing the spiritual cosmic music through and beyond the external music of the physical world.

In the tenth and eleventh centuries, this relation between external, materialistic music, of which the divine origin was highlighted, and its heavenly prototype was still beautifully expressed. People were required to employ music as a form of sacrificial or religious service and were expected to free themselves of their connection with the purely chaotic and — as it was felt to be — impure outer world when they produced musical sounds. Life in ordinary external speech was felt to be impure. People felt themselves transported to spiritual heights when they elevated themselves from speech to music as the image of celestial music. This feeling was expressed in the following words:

Ut queant laxis
*re*sonare fibris
*mi*ra gestorum

*fa*muli tuorum
*so*lve polluti
*la*bii reatum,
S.J. (*Sancte Johanne*)

We might translate this as follows: 'So that thy servants may sing with liberated vocal chords the wonder of thy works, pardon the sins of the lips which have become earthly—one might say which have become capable of speech—O Saint John.' It was to one who could hear the heavenly Jerusalem that men looked up in this connection. Let us extract certain things that lie hidden in such a verse: *Ut* (this word was later replaced by doh), resonare (*re*), mira (*mi*), famuli (*fa*), solve (*sol*), labii (*la*), S.J. (*si*). So you find that 'doh, re, mi, fa, sol, la, si', the names of the notes in medieval musical notation, have been carefully hidden in this verse. In such an instance we can go back to what still lived in human minds right until the eleventh or twelfth centuries through atavistic clairvoyant cognition, and we see how it all disappears in the flood of materialistic attitudes and passes out of human awareness. But now we are living at a time when through spiritual knowledge we must find it again and recreate it. Everything points clearly to the way in which evolution has made a descent so deep that a swamp has formed. The muddy water of this morass is made up of all the ideas originating in a materialistic view of the world. And now we are about to struggle up again out of the swamp of materialism, to ascend and rediscover what humankind has lost in its descent.

I have pointed out that, properly speaking, we do not only sleep by night but that certain parts of our being also sleep by day. At night it is principally the thinking and feeling parts which sleep, while during the day it is more the willing and feeling parts which sleep. It is in this will sphere that we are submerged when we dive down with the ego into the astral body. And when we hear a musical work, what happens is that we consciously dive down with our ego into the part of us which is otherwise asleep. When you sit and listen to a symphony, the inner process which takes place is a dulling of your ordinary, everyday thought life while you plunge with soul and spirit down into a region which otherwise sleeps during daytime consciousness. This brings about the connection between the effect of music and all the life-giving forces in the human organism, all that streams with living force through the whole human being, letting him grow together as one with the flowing volume of sounds.

And at night, when we sleep, our ordinary thought life is dulled in an element which as yet is not present in our normal consciousness. I have just said that when we experience music the ego's awareness dives down into a region which sleeps during the day. But if we succeed in bringing into ordinary everyday consciousness that which awakens when we sleep, if that in which we live when asleep dives down into our waking experience, if we submerge what we experience at night into the consciousness of daytime, then poetry arises. This is what people like Plato[11] felt when they called poetry a 'divine dreaming'.

When we thus explore the connection that exists between the human being and the whole cosmos, which we can do to a certain extent under the guidance of art, we can bring a certain measure of life into what otherwise remains a mere skeleton of ideas. Please do realize that these things are not a mere skeleton! Some people take such pleasure in arranging what I have described in my book *Theosophy* in the pattern of a diagram; no doubt they thought that it was from pure obstinacy that I deviated from the pattern of earlier theosophical teachings when I described three threefold organizations that are not separate but interlaced. But if these matters are approached through what one experiences and what is absolutely real, then even the nature of major and minor melodies will show that things are deeply rooted in the whole structure of the cosmos. Only when things are taken as living entities out of the whole structure of the cosmos do they correspond to a true reality.

Of course it was necessary in the beginning to say a number of things, the reasons for which have only gradually become apparent during the course of many years. This naturally involved the risk that people would start to criticize because they did not know the basis on which certain statements were made, how things of necessity present themselves when the whole structure of the cosmos is taken into consideration. This is still the case in many matters. Many things that are said now are open to numerous objections if they are approached on the basis of superficial knowledge. But in the course of years, even decades, they will certainly be verified. And the knowledge gained through spiritual science will become fruitful as soon as it is no longer a theory but a living experience.

It all depends upon the capacity to surmount the initial ideas generated by the terms physical body, etheric body, astral body, etc., so that these ideas can become alive; a real understanding of the universe radiates from this process of bringing them to life. Those who are able to do so should now compare the kind of aesthetics that have come to the fore during the last century and a half with what can be learned from a knowledge of the human being in discovering the origin of the arts. Those who make this comparison will see that unless there is an understanding of the human organization it is impossible to reach a real comprehension of what exists around us and gives us joy.

I want to awaken in you a recognition of the fact that spiritual science is itself an initial impulse that will continue to grow and develop, that we are in a sense called upon to make the very first steps, and that we can imagine what these first steps will lead to long after we have laid aside our bodies in our present incarnation.

Buddhi — wisdom of the human being, of the soul and of the spirit

Spiritual science can tell us what it is that acts thus in the etheric body. It is what corresponds today to what human beings will develop in a far distant future as Spirit Man, or Atma. At present, the human being does not possess this Atma as his own. It is bestowed upon him by the surrounding outer spiritual world, without his being able to participate in it. Later on, in the distant future, he will himself have developed it within him. That which saturates the etheric body, then, is Spirit Man, or Atma, and at the present stage of human evolution it is in a sense a superhuman being.

This superhuman Atma, or Spirit Man, expresses itself by contracting the etheric body—cramping it, as it were. Using an analogy from the sense world, we can compare the effect to that of frost, which cramps and contracts the physical body. The human being is as yet not ripe for what one day will be his most precious possession, and therefore, in a sense, it destroys him. The result of the contraction described above is that the astral element is pressed out, squeezed out. As the etheric body is compressed, the physical body as well is proportionately subjected to tension, whereby the astral body makes room for itself. You can visualize it approximately by imagining a sponge being squeezed. Now, the activities in the astral body are all emotional experiences—pleasure, distaste, joy, sorrow—and this process of being squeezed communicates itself to sentience as the sense of life. This is the process that takes place in the astral body, and it expresses itself as a feeling of freedom, strength, lassitude, etc.

Now let us ascend a bit. We listed the sense of our own movements as the second sense. In this case, again, an extraneous principle is at work in the etheric body, and again it is one not yet indigenous in the human being. He has not achieved it through his own efforts, it flows into him out of the spiritual world, and, as with Atma, the etheric body is saturated with it as a sponge with water. It is the Life Spirit, or Buddhi, which in time will permeate him, but which for the present he holds as a gift from the Life Spirit of the world. Its action is different from that of Atma. As water seeks its level, so Buddhi effects proportion, equilibrium in the etheric and physical bodies, and hence in the astral body as well. This condition operates in such a way that when the balance is disturbed it can re-establish itself automatically. If we stretch out an arm, for example, destroying the balance through this change of position, the balance is immediately restored because the astral body is in a state of equilibrium. As we stretch out an arm, the astral current streams proportionately in the opposite direction, thereby readjusting the balance. With every physical change of position, even merely blinking, the astral current in the organism moves in the opposite direction. The sense of movement manifests itself in this inner experience of a process of equalization.

We come now to a third element that can permeate the human being's etheric body, and this, too, is something that has entered human consciousness only to a negligible extent: Manas, or Spirit Self. But inasmuch as it is incumbent upon human beings to develop Manas in the present age, this being their earth task, Manas acts differently upon the etheric body than do Atma and Buddhi,

which are to be developed in the distant future. Its action
is to expand the etheric body, creating the opposite effect
to what we described as 'frost' in connection with the
sense of life. This activity could be compared with a
pouring, a streaming, of warmth into space, and it
expands the elastic etheric body. We have something like
streaming warmth when this semi-conscious expansion in
the etheric body occurs. The consequence of such elastic
expansion of the etheric body is a corresponding rarefac-
tion of the astral body, which can thus expand as well. It
need not be squeezed out; by having more room it can
remain in the expanding etheric body. While the sense of
life becomes conscious through the contraction of the
astral body, the static sensation results from the expansion
of the etheric body, which thus makes more room for the
astral body. By way of a comparison we can say that the
texture of the astral body becomes rarefied, less dense.
Such thinning of the etheric and the astral bodies offers the
possibility for the physical body to expand as well—to
extend itself in a sense. Through the action of Atma the
physical body is contracted, through the action of Buddhi
it is stabilized, through the action of Manas it is unbur-
dened. The result is that at certain points it pushes out tiny
particles, and this occurs in those three marvellous organs,
the semicircular canals of the ear. Such spreading out of
physical matter does not arise as the result of force exerted
from within, but as the result of a cessation or reduction of
pressure from without, through the release of pressure on
physical matter. This in turn enables the astral body to

expand more and more. It makes contact with the outer world and must achieve equilibrium with it, for when this is not the case we cannot stand upright, indeed we fall over. If we want to move in space we must take our bearings, and for this reason those three little canals are arranged in the three dimensions of space at right angles to each other.

About the essence of the gesture

If eurythmy represents the revelation of the human being through the fully developed gesture, then it must be differentiated from mime on the one hand and dance on the other. Eurythmy does not wish to be either of those things. The aim of eurythmy is to represent in the movement of the individual human limb or the whole human being what language represents in the air formed by the human organism. And eurythmy was indeed created in such a way that the same impulses that the human organism transfers into the formed air as a mediator of language or song are translated into movement. As a consequence, eurythmy cannot be interpreted intellectually, but the shape of each individual movement, each gesture must be understood artistically. And the more we approach a eurythmy performance artistically without an intellectual interpretation, the more we will learn to understand eurythmy. For just as the young child draws human language out of the essence of the human organism, albeit unconsciously, so eurythmy is drawn out as visible language or visible song from the same human organism — although no less elementary, no less subject to the inner laws because it is done consciously.

And it is, basically, the same thing as eurythmy, which is formed when we speak or sing: a gesture, simply a gesture, which is formed in the exhaled stream of air through the way that the air flow is shaped. Take an *A* (ah), for example, as a component of language. Essentially, *A* as an expression of a soul element communicates something like wonder or amazement. But if *A* occurs in the context of language such a feeling of wonder or amazement is diluted, fuses with the other elements in the word and in language. People no longer reflect on, let alone feel something of what originally flowed from the feeling element of their being into the *A*. As a gesture in the air, the *A* is formed by a full stream of breath flowing to the outside, taking on what we might describe as a concave shape, retreating from the existing density of the outside air as it flows out.

If a person speaks an *E* (ay), it is as if his speech organs were to produce a kind of dam. The exhaled stream of air initially pours into the outside world with full force but is then stopped, dammed up by the density of the external air and divides.

When we speak an *I*, we create it very much at the front, giving it a force which runs towards a point. We express *I* in such a way that it enters the density of the external air like an arrow, splitting the external air, we might say, like a sword. When we speak an *O*, it is as if in a certain sense we simultaneously hold back the air as we expel it, so that we work on the external air with the air we expel, thus forming something like a bearing into the external air.

With the *U*, it is as if we split the external air and experience the *U* in the recombination of the two external streams of air. And thus we can observe the air gesture in looking at the form which the air takes in producing a sound.

We can see this in the vowels, as I have just explained, and we can also see it in the consonants, can see it in the way that people express the soul element in words, in the combination of sentences as speech elements and song elements.

If all these things are then experienced inwardly in an artistic way and transferred to human movement, particularly the movement of the arms and hands, visible speech or song arises. And we then achieve a very special relationship with what is revealed to the eye as speech and what in normal speech or song is revealed to the ear in hearing. Human beings are organized such that the rest of the organism remains unused when we speak or sing and only a part of the rhythmical, the respiratory and heart organism is used as a basis which sends its forces into the head. The organism of the head is then the main source for what lives in the word or in the singing voice. And everything that comes from the human heart must penetrate what we reveal through speech, through singing in such a way that only a reflection, an echo of that experience of the heart, of the feelings penetrates speech and song. The reason why this must be so is that in the end the whole of the human organism in its capacity as head organism is organized in such a way that the things that are expressed through the head are adapted to fit in with physical life. The human being, really a child of the cosmos, separates himself from the cosmic context in that his head organism is fully adapted to physical conditions. And since the head organism, in turn, continues to live in speech and song, and in a sense only receives the impulses from the rhythmical element from below, human beings, when they express themselves in speech or song, are essentially physical beings existing between birth and death.

As a consequence, everything that human beings are when they detach themselves from the weight of physical existence must be placed between the sounds and tones in writing poetry or composing songs. When we take language into account, the poet must make the heart speak in the way he uses onomatopoeia, in the way he lightens or darkens one sound with another, in the way he brings the musical rhythm or beat or a musical theme to life — not through what lives in the prose sounds but through what lives musically in the sequence of sounds. In this sense it would be true to say that the heart does not live in the sounds but in the relationship between the individual sounds, in the movement of the stream of sound. What the poet achieves in the way he handles a sentence or verse can already be expressed in the way that the individual gestures for the sounds themselves are formed in the visible speech of eurythmy. Furthermore, what is to be expressed in the language of eurythmy and comes to expression in these movements is pushed back into the human soul element. Every time we speak a word containing the sound *A*, for example, when we say grass for instance, wonder or amazement underlies the full experience of the word grass, influenced by the other sounds. Every time we vocalize, revelations of the soul, such as wonder, are indicated.

But those feeling elements alive in speech are stripped off in language which has become a conventional expression of thinking in a time which lacks artistic feeling—language itself has turned strongly prosaic. All those feeling elements are fully reawakened when the possibilities of visible human expression that otherwise only appear in the most rudimentary form are revealed in the articulated gestures and soul qualities of eurythmy. That is why the things which come to expression in poetry and eurythmy, which we can present in recitation and declamation accompanied by a different instrument than the human larynx and other speech organs (i.e. if we recite or declaim and at the same time do eurythmy), are like the orchestral harmonies of two different instruments which only in their very different revelation bring the rich content of true artistic creation to expression.

When eurythmy is undertaken with recitation, this is basically something that is experienced artistically in the soul through the interaction of both. We can therefore accompany eurythmy with recitation and declamation in such a way that the latter are in turn artistically presented, as happened in ages that were more artistically inclined than the present one. Because we have little artistic feeling today, it is mostly the case that the prosaic element in recitation and declamation is merely given somewhat greater emphasis. Such an approach basically lacks any poetic artistry. Something artistic only occurs in poetry if hidden eurythmy is already contained in recitation and declamation. It only occurs if in the artistic recitation and declamation of sounds, in the movement that lies in the sequence of sounds, everything is awoken that is inner movement of soul, elevation or depression of soul and so on — when everything that lies between the sounds and in the movement of the sounds is taken into account in the treatment of speech and not the stress on particular words.

The difference between dance and eurythmy can be understood more clearly when we play music in an orchestra or on an instrument and accompany that with eurythmy. In this situation we are not dealing with dance, but with song which, however, comes to expression in movement and not in sound. The difference between eurythmy, accompanied by music, and dance is that in eurythmy everything is pushed back into the impulses generating the movements of the person, which are grasped with full consciousness, so that it is actually the soul which moves in the limbs, whereas in dance the soul gives itself over to the limbs and the limbs then create the required form in space. Hence a person will lose himself in the movements of dance whereas in eurythmy, when it accompanies music, he will reveal the foundations of his soul and spirit. It is therefore eurythmy which most truly takes hold of the inward nature of the human being in comparison both to mime, which can also accompany speech and is therefore indicative, and to dance. If we allow eurythmy to work on us in a real artistic way, we have to say that in ordinary speech, even when used for poetry, in truth only a shadow of the heart speaks through the head. Eurythmy calls the heart to speak through the whole human being and suppresses handling speech as mere thought, something that is actually inartistic.

We might put it like this, that we observe the movement which is otherwise only concentrated in the heart — the movement of the human life-giving element, the blood — and we perceive what occurs in the motion, the weaving and flowing of the blood as a whole when we speak. And what in other circumstances human beings first take into the physical organ of the heart, transferring it from there to the soul as excitement so that it flows into the word, that element flows directly into the person's movement. So we might say: it is one thing to trace what ebbs and flows in the movement of the air when a person speaks artistically, to trace that right into the heart so that the heart manifests everywhere in its movement, in its beat as an echo of the soul. If that were directly traced and, on the other hand, if we traced what we now attempt to guide to the outside instead of into the heart — if that were traced in the forms of the arm movements or in the forms of the whole human being in space, we should actually discover in the artistic experience on the wings of such a eurythmy movement the heart flowing out into the cosmos from the human being. It is the heart dedicating itself to the world, so to speak, that lives in eurythmy.

All these things are, of course, still in their beginning stages today. But so many possibilities lie in the development of the movements which are to be revealed through such advances that we may truly hope that the art of eurythmy will one day, when it is fully developed, come to reveal the nature of the human being, which itself is an instrument of this art. One day, eurythmy will be able to take its rightful place as a younger art alongside the rightful older arts. That is why today we must still ask the audience for its forbearance, but an interest can certainly be aroused as does happen and has always happened at the rise of a new art form.

Movement: the speech of the soul

Eurythmy — of which we will now see a performance — represents the endeavour to create from the possibilities of movement inherent in the human organism, which are then carried over into the movement of a group of people, something that to begin with appears to be elaborated gesture. On the stage you will see in the movement of one person or a group of people something that seems, at first sight, to be gesture. Only in eurythmy, gesture becomes actual speech.

Now before a small child begins to express his soul life as he forms the sounds of speech, he babbles, and this babbling only later on becomes articulate speech. In ordinary life, we find that when human beings realize a need to impart more inner intensity to the sounds of speech they accompany these sounds with gesture. This makes the sounds more personal and intimate in character, filled in greater measure with the quality of soul.

These gestures—which proceed purely from the realm of instinctive feeling—are thus a kind of 'babbling expressed in movement', and they can be developed and elaborated. Just as the babbling of a little child is a gradual revelation of his soul, so we can elaborate to the point of actual speech the gestures made with varying degrees of emphasis by different people according to whether they want to create a more personal or impersonal effect.

Such gestures, of course, cannot be elaborated in an arbitrary way. We cannot simply take the meaning or content of certain words and then proceed to express this content in movement, for such movement could never be really expressive. It would be just as if we were to do exactly what we liked with speech and imagined that we could substitute the sound *I* for *A* according to the mood of soul in the word. The movement must reveal the actual experience of the soul, just as each sound—whether it be a vowel or a consonant—brings to expression an experience of the soul. In advanced languages, however, speech has departed very far from its original source; and this is the very reason why we have so many languages. We can invariably recognize that simple, primitive sounds are the expression of certain quite definite experiences of the soul.

'Ah!' has remained as an expression of wonder, astonishment; the sound *e* (eh) as an expression of disturbance, and so on. And just as the vowels — expressing inner experiences of the soul — reveal the realm of feeling, so the consonants imitate outer happenings, outer existence. In this respect, our speech is a continual interweaving of what, in the consonants, we imitate from without. That includes everything that arises in our feeling and perception in relation to outer events, events which we meet with sympathy, antipathy or intermediate shades of feeling.

Now just as in speech a sound, a phrase, the turning of a phrase, a question, an exclamation, an ordinary statement or, in poetry rhythm, measure, rhyme correspond to experiences of the soul, so we can find in exactly the same way an expression of the human organism in movement. Moreover this movement can be just as unequivocal as the sound itself. Here we have one kind of eurythmy — speech eurythmy.

We also have tone eurythmy, where the faculties of movement inherent in the human organism become visible song. In speech eurythmy, the movements corresponding to the sounds are carried out by one person in a group and are accompanied by recitation or declamation. Tone eurythmy — visible song — is accompanied by instrumental music. And just as every sound, combination of sound, every structure and form of a phrase is an expression of the soul in speech eurythmy, so every tone, musical phrase, melody, rhythm and harmony can be expressed as visible song. Along these lines we can develop an art that speaks in a definite language of forms using the human being himself as an instrument and, moreover, doing so in such a way that the human being translates into harmonious movement the elements of his being, which we may describe as form at rest.

Now if we study the inner possibilities of expression of this human form at rest, we are led to sculpture. Unprejudiced perception beholds the silent soul in everything that is thus given plastic form in space. As a matter of fact, any sculpture that does not aim at expressing the permanent qualities of the soul — temperament, character, the whole inner condition of the human being, in short that which has come to comparative rest in the soul — is not true to its nature if it attempts to give expression to a momentary movement of the soul. It is inconsistent for the art of sculpture to attempt to express anything that is not the silent soul, the soul at rest in itself.

If, on the other hand, we would portray the speaking, articulate soul, we must use the human being himself as an instrument, realizing that all form in human beings is striving perpetually to become movement. The form of the human hand at rest is really a contradiction in itself; the human hand is always striving to enter into movement. The outstretched hand already has within it, in embryo, the pointing hand, the beckoning hand. The moment the hand at rest becomes the beckoning or grasping hand — in that moment the movement made by the human being becomes an expression of the speaking soul, just as the forms of sculpture are an expression of the silent soul.

The human being contains the whole cosmos within himself. Our observation is poor in content if we have eyes only for earthly conditions. Around us is the world; within us is the sum total of our thoughts and ideas to which our feelings adhere. We might conceivably hear someone say: 'Take a man who has a great knowledge of the world, one who has attentively observed his whole environment. I, too, look at his environment and if I were in a position to look by some means into his soul, I should find a "soul-photograph" of the environment.' In short, all that lives in the thoughts of the human being is a soul photograph of his environment. Now there is a great deal more in the human being than his thoughts, despite the seeming contradiction. The human being is an 'organization'. He appears, in the first place, as a physical being. But is the physical element really the essential thing about him? In our materialistic age we think it is, but that is just the same as if I were to gaze at a coloured picture, looking here for violet, there for brownish purple, examining all its details and then proceed to describe how the blue lies above the violet, the yellow under the green and so forth. This is not the essential thing at all; the essential thing is what is being expressed in the picture. The material is not the essential element.

The same thing holds good when we observe the human being as a physical being. The way in which modern science looks at a person is childishly naive. The human organization, regarded as a picture, is an expression of the whole universe. The ideas in our soul, in our mind — so-called — express the physical world around us. If we could but rightly observe our physical being, we should realize that it is an expression of the whole universe. The human being is a microcosm — and the microcosm is form. If a person brings this microcosm into movement, if he expresses all that is living in his form by letting it pass over into movement — then the whole divine-spiritual cosmos is speaking through him as its instrument. The human being is a little world, a microcosm, in relation to the great world, the macrocosm.

Compared with the great work of creation, art in its activity is a creation in miniature. And this creation in miniature may be accomplished most worthily of all when its instrument is one which contains all cosmic secrets, all cosmic laws, namely, the human being. And so, when movement is released from the human form at rest (expressing the silent soul), when we succeed in allowing form to pass over into movement in eurythmy, all cosmic secrets can be expressed. If a true poet desires to give expression to cosmic secrets, a kind of hidden eurythmy is already there in his words. When eurythmy is accompanied by declamation and recitation, emphasis must not be laid on the prose content of the poem; nor must the aim of the reciter be to infuse feelings and emotions into his recitation and declamation, for that is not artistic, it is merely artificial. In our modern materialistic age there is such a strong desire to saturate the prose content of a poem in recitation and declamation with emotion, enthusiasm, ardour and the like. In true art this is impossible. What we must realize is that imaginations are actually expressed by the sounds used by the poet, and that music or the sculptural principle lies in his treatment of language. All this must be expressed in recitation. Then a true, quick rhythm, for instance, will of itself express all that is revealed by a particular feeling; a slow rhythm will express something different. When melody enters into language, the whole range of feelings will be introduced by the way the language is handled, not by an artificial infusion of emotion.

A hidden eurythmy is contained in the very way in which the poet handles his language and this hidden eurythmy must also be expressed in recitation and declamation. And so it is that eurythmy aims at bringing visible song and speech into being. When we see tone eurythmy, which is accompanied by instrumental music, the difference between dancing and something that is 'sung' in movement and not 'danced' is quite apparent. If we recognize the difference between tone eurythmy and dancing, we shall at once realize the aim of tone eurythmy and also begin to understand what speech eurythmy is striving to become.

It is of course obvious that in our age, when people are so opposed to anything new, there will not be much understanding of eurythmy nor of the new kind of declamation and recitation. We know all this, but we also know that we have the beginning here of a definite impulse of development in art — a development that will only become fully apparent in the future.

On the other hand we know that only a beginning has as yet been made. We ourselves are our severest critics and we realize all the objections that may justifiably arise.

Moreover, we pay attention to them because we are striving to reach greater and greater perfection. Only a short time ago, a course of lectures on tone eurythmy was given in the school with the object of taking our work a step forward. When people say glibly that all our aims are already contained in the other arts and that speech can quite well be left as it is, this shows that they have no true feeling for art. In those who have, there is inevitably the longing for an expansion and development in the domain of art.

Out of such a longing — a longing to develop art along lines in harmony with its deepest origin — tone and speech eurythmy have come into being. And that is why we are convinced that a greater and greater understanding of eurythmy will grow up in the hearts of all who are possessed of true artistic feeling. Anastasius Grün[12] once wrote these beautiful words: 'When will the last poet be living? He will be living even when earth herself is facing its end, for so long as there is life on earth, so long will there be poetry.' So long, too, will there be art, and feeling for art. We are convinced of this. So long as human beings have any artistic feeling, so long will there be delight in any expansion of art. Eurythmy, indeed, has come forth from this desire for and delight in an expansion of art. And thus we dare hope that eurythmy, taking its place among the other arts, will play a real part in their development and growth.

The Cloud Illuminator

Note at the side of the text of *Der Wolkendurchleuchter* (The Cloud Illuminator): 'To develop the feeling and mood of veneration and to achieve peace'.

Lory Maier-Smits, 'the first eurythmist', relates the following. The next part of the presentation was devoted to making personal pronouns visible. Lory had examples for 'I', 'you' and 'we'. There were many variations of lemniscates carried out together in a circle. And then it was discovered that Lory had forgotten the forms for 'he'.

This turned out to be a stroke of luck! Rudolf Steiner only said, 'I see, what you are lacking are texts. I will provide them for you.' After a reflective silence, which the participants must have experienced as a truly creative pause, he asked the three oldest people present to form a small circle at the centre of the room. Then he spoke in a strong, ringing voice the first verse ever created for eurythmy:

> He who illuminates the clouds,
> May he illuminate,
> May he irradiate,
> May he inspire,
> And fill with warmth and light
> Even me.[13]

In doing so, he also directed their steps. During the first line, reverently take two steps backwards, forming a larger circle. During the four supplications, move around the circle with anapaestic steps. During the last line approach the circle's centre again, the divine. They repeated it several times. Everyone was deeply impressed. This was an experience of the lofty tasks which eurythmy would be able to take up in the future.

A lecture on eurythmy

Eurythmy has grown up out of the soil of the anthroposophical movement,[14] and the history of its origin
makes it almost appear to be a gift of the forces of destiny.
In 1912, the Anthroposophical Society[15] lost one of its
members,[16] the father of a family, and as a result it was
necessary for his daughter to choose a profession; a profession, however, which could be found within the field of
anthroposophical activity. After much thought, it seemed
possible to make this the opportunity for the inauguration
of a new art of movement in space, different from anything which had arisen up to that time.

And thus, out of the teaching given to this young girl,[17]
there arose the very first principles and movements of
eurythmy.

Eurythmy must be seen as one of the many activities
arising out of the anthroposophical movement which have
grown up in such a way that their origins must be looked
upon as the result of the workings of destiny. I spoke some
days ago about the forms of the pillars of the
Goetheanum[18] and mentioned how I had stood before
these pillars and realized that through artistic activity they
had gained a life of their own, and had developed quite
different qualities from those with which they had
originally been endowed.

The same may be said about the art of eurythmy. This is
always the case when one draws upon the creative forces
of nature, either in one's work as an artist or in any other

form of human activity. Just as the creative forces of nature draw upon the inexhaustible source of the infinite, so that it is always possible to perceive in something that has come to fruition much more than was originally implanted in it, so is it also when artistic impulses unite themselves with the mighty creative forces of nature. In such a case the artist is not merely developing some more or less limited impulse, but he reaches the point when he makes of himself an instrument for the creative powers of the universe, so that very much more grows out of his activity than he could originally have intended or foreseen.

At the time of which I speak, eurythmy was studied only by a very few people. At the beginning of the war [First World War], Frau Dr Steiner undertook their further training, and from that time on eurythmy became more and more widely known, and its artistic possibilities very much enriched. The art of eurythmy, as we know it today, has developed out of the first principles which were given in the year 1912. The work since then has been carried on without interruption; but eurythmy is still only in its first beginnings, and we are working unceasingly towards its further development and perfection.

I am, however, convinced that eurythmy bears within it infinite possibilities, and that in the future, when those who were responsible for its inauguration will long have left their work in other hands, eurythmy will develop further until it is able to take its place as a younger art by the side of those other arts having an older tradition.

No art has ever risen out of human intention intellectually conceived, neither can the principle of imitating nature ever produce an art. On the contrary, true art has always been born out of human hearts able to open themselves to the impulses coming from the spiritual world, human hearts which felt compelled to realize these impulses and to embody them in some way in external matter.

It can be seen how, in the case of each separate art — architecture, for example, sculpture, painting or music — certain spiritual impulses were poured into humanity from higher worlds. These impulses were taken up by certain individuals specially fitted to receive them, and in this way, through human activity, pictures of the higher worlds were reflected in the physical world; and the various arts came into being.

It is true that the arts, in the course of their further development, have for the most part become naturalistic, and have lost their connection with the impulses that originally inspired them, a mere imitation of external nature taking their place. Such imitation, however, could never be the source of any true art.

Today, when a sculptor or painter wishes to represent the human figure, he does so by studying and working from a model. It can, however, easily be shown that the art of sculpture, which reached its zenith during the civilization of ancient Greece, did not arise through the artist working from a model, and in this way more or less imitating the external impressions of the senses. At that time, when the plastic art of Greece was in full bloom, human beings were still to some extent aware of the etheric body, which contains within it the formative forces and the forces of growth. At the height of Greek civilization,[19] human beings knew how to make use of the etheric body when bringing an arm or hand, for instance, into a certain attitude, and the position and arrangement of the muscles were an actual experience to them. They had an inner understanding of the possibilities of movement in the arm and hand, of the possibilities of muscular expansion and contraction. And they were able to bring this inner experience to physical expression, making use of physical materials.

Thus the Greek sculptor incorporated into matter a real, inward experience, not merely the external impression of the eye. He did not say to himself 'the lines go in this or that direction', and then proceed to embody in plastic form the perceptions of his physical senses; but for him it was indeed an actual inward experience which he recreated out of the creative forces of nature, and entrusted to external physical matter.

This is true of every form of art. There have always been and will always be, in the course of human evolution on the earth, epochs during which art is at its height, during which influences from the spiritual worlds penetrate more easily into the souls of human beings than at other times, urging them to turn their gaze towards the spiritual worlds and to carry down from there living spiritual impulses. This is how every true art is brought to birth.

Such periods of civilization are always followed by others of a more naturalistic tendency, in which certain arts often achieve greater external perfection than they had possessed at an earlier stage; but this perfection bears within it traces of decadence, whereas in their beginnings these arts were permeated with a more vital, a more powerful and enthusiastic spiritual impulse. At that earlier stage they had not yet lost their true reality; their technique was the outcome of the whole human being. It was not a merely external, traditional technique, but was based on the body, soul and spirit of the human being.

The realization of this fact of human evolution might well give one courage to develop ever further such an art of eurythmy, which has been borne on the wings of fate into the anthroposophical movement. For it is the task of the anthroposophical movement to reveal to our present age that spiritual impulse which is suited to it.

I speak in all humility when I say that within the anthroposophical movement there is a firm conviction that a spiritual impulse of this kind must now, at the present time, enter once more into human evolution. And this spiritual impulse must, among its other means of expression, embody itself in a new form of art. It will increasingly be realized that this particular form of art has been given to the world in eurythmy.

It is the task of anthroposophy to bring a greater depth, a wider vision and a more living spirit into the other forms of art. But the art of eurythmy could only grow up out of the soul of anthroposophy, could only receive its inspiration through a purely anthroposophical conception. It is through speech that the human being is able to reveal his inner being outwardly to his fellow human beings. Through speech he can most easily disclose his inmost nature.

At all periods of civilization, in a form suited to the particular epoch, side by side with those arts which need for their expression either the external element of space or the external element of time, accompanying and completing these, we find that art which manifests itself through speech — the art of poetry.

The art of speech — I purposely use the expression 'the art of speech' to describe poetry, and the justification for doing so will appear later — is more comprehensive and universal than the other arts, for it can embody other forms of art within its own form. It can be said that the art of poetry is an art of speech which in the case of one poet works more sculpturally, and in the case of another more musically. Indeed one can go so far as to say that painting itself can enter into the art of poetry.

Speech is a universal means of expression for the human soul. And anyone who is able to gaze with unprejudiced vision into the earliest times of human evolution on earth can see that in certain primeval languages a really fundamental artistic element entered into human evolution. Such primeval languages were, however, drawn out of the whole human organization to a far greater degree than is the case with modern languages.

When one investigates without prejudice the course of

the evolution of the human being, one discovers certain ancient languages that might almost be likened to song. Such singing was, however, enhanced by accompanying movements of the legs and arms, so that a kind of dancing was added. This was especially the case when a solemn form of expression was sought, the form of some ritual or cult.

In those primeval times of human evolution the accompanying of the word which issued forth from the larynx with gesture and movement was felt to be something absolutely natural. It is only possible to gain a true understanding of what lies behind these things, when one realizes that what otherwise appears only as gesture accompanying speech can gain for itself independent life. It will then become apparent that movements which are carried out by the arms and hands can be not merely equally expressive from the artistic point of view, but much more expressive than speech itself.

It must be admitted that such an unprejudiced attitude with regard to these things is not always to be found. One often observes a certain antipathy towards the accompanying of speech by gesture. Indeed, I myself have noticed that certain people even go so far as to consider it not in very good taste when a speaker accompanies his discourse with pronounced gesture. As a result of this the habit has grown up, and is by no means unusual in the present day, of putting one's hands in one's pockets when making a speech. I must say that I have always found this attitude most unsympathetic.

It is a fact that the inmost nature of the human being can be revealed most wonderfully through movements of the arms and hands. My fingers often itch to take up my pen and write an essay on the philosopher Franz Brentano,[20] a dear friend of mine who died some years ago. I have already written a good deal about him, but I should much like to write yet another essay, based on what I shall now relate.

When Franz Brentano mounted the platform and took his place at the lectern, he was himself the embodiment of his entire philosophy, the spiritual content of which called forth such deep admiration when clothed in philosophical terms and concepts.

Brentano's philosophy, in itself, was far more beautiful than his own description of it. All that he could say in words was revealed through the way in which he moved his arms and hands while speaking, through the way in which he held out the piece of paper containing the notes of his lecture. It was a very remarkable type of movement, and its most striking characteristic was that by means of this piece of paper and, indeed, by his whole attitude he gave the impression of imparting something of great significance, while at the same time preserving an appearance of unconcern. So that in the course of one of his lectures one could see his entire philosophy expressed in these many different gestures.

What is especially interesting about Franz Brentano is the fact that he founded a psychology in which he departs from the theories of other psychologists, such as

Spencer,[21] Stuart Mill[22] and others, by refusing to include
the will among the psychological categories. I am
acquainted with all that Franz Brentano brought forward
to substantiate this theory of his, but I found nothing so
convincing as the way in which he held his piece of paper.
The instant he began to make gestures with his hands and
arms, all trace of will disappeared from his whole bearing
as a philosopher, while feeling and idea revealed themselves in the most remarkable manner. This pre-
ponderance of idea and feeling, and the disappearance of
will, underlay every movement that he made with his
hands. So that one day I shall really find myself compelled
to write an essay: 'The Philosophy of Franz Brentano, as
revealed through his gesture and bearing'. For it seems to
me that much more was expressed in these gestures than
in any philosophical discourse on the subject.

Those who enter deeply and without prejudice into this
matter will gradually realize that the breath which we
expel from our lungs, our organs of speech and song,
when vocalized and given form by means of the lips, teeth
and palate is really nothing else than gestures in the air.
Only in this case these air gestures are projected into space
in such a way that they conjure up sounds which can be
heard by the ear.

If we succeed with true sensory and supersensory
vision in penetrating into the nature of these air gestures,
into all that the human being actually does when he utters
a vowel or consonant sound, when he forms sentences,
uses rhyme and rhythm, the iambus[23] or trochee[24] — when

we penetrates into these gestures of the air, the thought arises that the languages of modern civilization have indeed made terrible concessions to convention. They have become simply a means of expression for scientific knowledge, a means of communicating the things of everyday life. They have lost their primeval spirituality.

Modern language bears out what has been so beautifully expressed by the poet: 'Spricht die Seele, // so spricht ach schon die Seele nicht mehr' ['Alas, when the soul speaks, in reality it speaks no more'].[25]

Now all that can be perceived by supersensory vision, all that can thus be learned about the nature of these forms and gestures of the air, can be carried into movements of the arms and hands, into movements of the whole human being. There then arises in visible form the actual counterpart of speech. One can use the entire human body in such a way that it really carries out those movements which are otherwise carried out by the organs connected with speech and music. Thus there arises visible speech, visible music—in other words, the art of eurythmy.

When one brings artistic feeling to the study of the nature of speech, one finds that the individual sounds form themselves into imaginative pictures. It is necessary, however, entirely to free oneself from the abstract character which language has assumed in the so-called advanced civilization of the present day. For it is an undeniable fact that when a modern person speaks he in no way brings his whole being into activity.

True speech, however, is born from the whole human

being. Let us take any one of the vowels. A vowel sound is always the expression of some aspect of the feeling life of the soul. The human being wishes to express what lives in his soul as wonder—Ah! Or holding himself upright against opposition—*A* (ā as in 'mate'); or the assertion of self, the consciousness of ego-existence in the world—*E* (e as in 'me'). Or again he wishes to express wonder, but now with a more intimate, caressing shade of feeling—*I*.

The character of the sounds is, of course, slightly different in the different languages, because each individual language proceeds from a differently constituted soul life. But every vowel sound does in its essence express some shade of the feeling life of the soul; and this feeling only has to unite itself with thought, with the head system, in order to pass over into speech.

What I have said about the vowel sounds of speech can be applied equally to the tones of music. The various sounds of speech, the use of idiom, the construction of phrases and sentences—all these things are the expression of the feeling life of the soul.

In singing also the soul life expresses itself through tone.

Let us now consider the consonants. The consonants are the imitation of what we find around us in external nature. The vowel is born out of the human being's inmost being; it is the channel through which this inner content of the soul streams outwards. The consonant is born out of the comprehension of external nature; the way in which we seize upon external things, even the way in which we perceive them with the eyes, all this is built into the form of the consonants. The consonant represents, paints, as it were, the things of the external world. In earlier times the consonants did actually contain within themselves a kind of imaginative painting of what exists in external nature.

Such things are, certainly, dealt with by many students of the science of language, but always in a one-sided manner. For instance, there exist two well-known theories with regard to the origin of language—the ding-dong theory[26] and the bow-wow theory[27]—which have been set out by researchers who are, as a matter of fact, absolutely lacking in any real understanding of their subject, but belong to that type of person who is constantly originating all sorts of scientific theories. The ding-dong theory is based upon the assumption that, as in the case of the bell, there lies some sort of a sound within every external object which is then imitated by the human being. Everything is included in this theory of imitation; and it has been named the ding-dong theory after the sound made by a bell, which is perhaps its most striking example. The idea is that when one says the word 'wave', one is imitating the actual movement of the waves—which is, indeed, perfectly true in this instance.

The other theory, the bow-wow theory, which could equally well be called the moo-moo theory, is one which assumes that speech in the first place arose from the transformation and development of the sounds of animals. And because one of the most striking of these sounds is 'bow-wow', this theory has been called the bow-wow theory.

Now all these theories do actually contain a certain element of truth. Scientific theories are never without some foundation. What is remarkable about them is that they do always contain say, a quarter, or an eighth, or a sixteenth, or a hundredth part of the truth; and it is this fraction of the truth, put forward as it is in a very clever and suggestive manner, which deceives people. The real truth is that the vowel arises from the soul life, and the consonant out of the perception and imitation of the external object. The human being imitates the external object through the way in which he holds back the stream of the breath with his lips, or gives it shape and form by means of the teeth, tongue and palate. While the consonants are formed in this way, by the fashioning of gestures in the air, the vowel sounds are the channel through which the inner soul life of the human being streams outwards.

The consonants give plastic form to what is to be expressed.

And in the same way as the single sounds, the single letters, are formed, so are sentences also formed, and poetic language becomes actual gesture in the air. Modern poetry, however, shows very clearly how the poet has to struggle against the abstract element in language.

As I have already said, our soul life does not in any way flow into the words which we speak; we do not enter into the sounds of speech with our inner being. How many of us really experience wonder, amazement, perplexity or the feeling of self-defence simply in the vowel sounds themselves. How many of us experience the soft, rounded surface of certain objects, the thrusting hammering nature of others, their angular or undulating, their velvety or prickly qualities, as these are expressed by the different consonants. And yet all these things are contained in speech.

If we follow the successive sounds as they occur in a single word, entering into the real nature of this word as it originally arose out of the whole being of the human being, then we can experience all possible shades of feeling, the ecstasy of joy, the depths of despair; we can experience the ascent and descent of the whole scale of the human emotions, the whole scale of the perception of external things.

All that I have been describing can be conjured up in imaginations in the same way as speech itself once came forth from the world of Imagination. One who has this imaginative vision perceives how the *E* sound (e as in 'me') always calls up in the soul a certain picture, a picture that expresses the assertion of self and shows how such self-assertion must be expressed through the stretching of the muscles, in the arm for example. Should anyone be able to use his nose in a skilful manner, he could also make an *E* with his nose! An *E* can also be shown by the direction in which the eye glances; but because the arms and hands are the most expressive part of the human body, it is more natural to make an *E* with the arms and it has a more beautiful effect. But the essential thing is that the stretching, penetrating feeling should really come to expression in *E*.

If we utter the sound *A* (ā as in 'mate') and take this outgoing stream of the breath as the prototype for the eurythmy movement, we find that the stream of air reveals itself to our Imagination as flowing in two crossed currents. This is how the eurythmy movement for *A* is derived. All these movements are just as little arbitrary in their nature as are the sounds of speech or the tones of music.

There are many people who are inclined to say that they have no wish for anything so hard and fast, that there should be more ways than one of expressing any particular sound in movement. They feel that the movements should arise quite spontaneously out of the human being. If, however, we desire such absolute spontaneity, we should carry this desire into the realm of speech itself and declare that there should be no German, French or English language to interfere with the freedom of the human being, but that each individual should feel himself at liberty to express himself by means of other sounds if he should so choose. It would be just as rational to say that the freedom of the human being is hindered through the fact that he must speak English or some other language.

But the existence of the different languages in no way interferes with human freedom. On the contrary, the human being could not express beauty in language if language were not already there to be used by him as an instrument, and in the same way beauty can only be expressed in the movements of eurythmy through the fact that eurythmy actually exists. Eurythmy in no way infringes upon human freedom. Such objections really arise from lack of insight.

Thus eurythmy has come into being as a visible language, using as its instrument the arms and hands which are undeniably the most expressive part of the whole human organism.

Today it should be possible to come to an understanding of these things by purely scientific means. Science, however, although on the right path with regard to much of the knowledge it has acquired, knows about as much of this matter as someone with a veal cutlet on his plate knows about a calf, namely, the most insignificant fraction. Scientists know that the centre of speech lies in the left region of the brain, and that this is connected with what the child acquires for himself by means of movement of the right arm. In the case of left-handed people the centre of speech is situated in the right side of the brain.

One might almost say that the scientist has no knowledge of the calf in its entirety, but is only acquainted with the veal cutlet! Thus he is aware only of the merest fraction of the whole connection between the life-processes in one or other arm and the origin of speech.

The truth is that speech itself arises out of those movements of the human limb system which are held back, and do not come to full expression. There could be no such thing as speech were it not for the fact that during the natural course of his early development the child has inherent within him the instinct to move his arms and hands. These movements are held back and become concentrated in the organs of speech; and the organs of speech are in themselves an image of that which seeks outlet in movements of the arms and hands, and in the accompanying movements of the other limbs.

The etheric body never uses the mouth as the vehicle of speech but invariably makes use of the limb-system. And it is those movements made by the etheric body during speech which are transferred into the physical body. Of course you can, if you choose, speak completely without gesture, even going so far as to stand rigidly still with your hands in your pockets; but in that case your etheric body will gesticulate all the more vigorously, out of sheer protest!

Thus you can see how, in very truth, eurythmy is drawn out of the human organization in just as natural a way as speech itself.

The poet has to fight against the conventionality of speech in order to be able to draw from speech that element which could make of it a way leading to the supersensory worlds. Thus the poet — if he is a true artist, which cannot be said of most of those people whose business it is to manufacture poems — does not over-emphasize the importance of the prose content of the words he uses. This prose content only provides him with the opportunity for expressing in words his true artistic impulse. Just as his material — the clay or the marble — is not the chief concern of the sculptor, but rather the inspiration that he is striving to embody in form, so the chief concern of the poet is the embodiment of his poetic inspiration in sounds that are imaginative, sculptural and musical.

And it is this artistic element which must be brought out in recitation and declamation.

In our somewhat inartistic age, it is customary in recitation and declamation to lay the chief stress on the prose content of a poem. Indeed, in these days, the mere fact of being able to speak at all is looked upon as sufficient ground for becoming a reciter. But the art of recitation and declamation should rank as highly as the other arts; for in recitation and declamation there is the possibility of treating speech in such a way that the hidden eurythmy lying within it, the imaginative, sculpted, coloured use of words, their music, rhythm and melody, are all brought to expression. When Goethe[28] was rehearsing his rhythmic dramas, he made use of a baton just as if he were the conductor of an orchestra; for he was not so much concerned with the merely prosaic content of the words, but with the bringing out of all that lay, like hidden eurythmy, in their construction and use.

Schiller[29] paid little heed when writing his most famous poems to the actual meaning of the words. For instance he wrote *Das Lied von der Glocke* [The Song of the Bell], but as far as the prose content of the words is concerned he might just as well have written a completely different poem. Schiller first experienced in his soul something that might be described as a vague musical motif, a sort of melody, and into this melody he wove his words like threaded pearls.

Language is truly poetic only in so far as it is used musically, sculpturally, or only in so far as it is filled with colour.

Frau Dr Steiner has devoted many years to the development of this special side of the art of recitation and declamation. It is her work which has made it possible to bind together into one artistic whole the picture presented on the stage by the 'visible speech' of eurythmy much in the same way as the various instruments of an orchestra are bound together—bind together what is expressed through a truly eurythmy treatment of speech, a truly eurythmy recitation and declamation.

So that, on the one hand, we have the visible speech of eurythmy and, on the other hand, the hidden eurythmy that lies not in tone production alone but in the whole way in which speech and language are treated. As far as the artistic element of poetry is concerned, the point is not that we say, 'The bird sings,' but that, paying due regard to what has gone before and to what is to come, we say with enthusiasm, for instance, 'The bird sings,' or again, in a more subdued tone of voice, at a quite different tempo, 'The bird sings.' Everything depends on giving due form and shape to the words and sentences. And it is just this which can be carried over into eurythmy, into our whole conception and treatment of eurythmy.

For this reason we must put before ourselves as an ideal this orchestral ensemble, this interplay between the visible art of eurythmy and the art of recitation and declamation.

Eurythmy cannot be accompanied by the ordinary

conventional recitation that is so well liked today. It would be impossible to do eurythmy to such an accompaniment because it is the soul qualities of the human being which must be given expression here, both audibly through speech and visibly through eurythmy.

Eurythmy can be accompanied not only by recitation and declamation but also by instrumental music. But here it must always be borne in mind that eurythmy is music translated into movement and is not dancing in any sense of the word. There is a fundamental difference between eurythmy and dancing. People, however, often fail to make this distinction when seeing eurythmy on the stage owing to the fact that eurythmy uses as its instrument the human body in motion. I myself know of a journalist—I am not personally acquainted with him, but his articles have been brought to my notice—who, writing on eurythmy, says: 'It cannot be denied that, when one witnesses a demonstration of eurythmy, the performers on the stage are continually in motion. Eurythmy must, therefore, be considered as dance and must be judged accordingly.' Now I think it will be admitted that what we have seen here of tone eurythmy, of this visible singing accompanied as it is by instrumental music, is clearly to be distinguished from ordinary dancing. Tone eurythmy is essentially something other than dance; it is a singing movement, a movement that can be carried out either by a single performer or by many together.

Although the movements of the arms and hands may be accompanied and amplified by movements of the other parts of the organism—the legs, for instance, or the head, the nose, ears, what you will—nevertheless these movements should only be used to strengthen the movement of the hands and arms in much the same way that we find means of emphasizing and strengthening the spoken word. If we wish to admonish a child we naturally put our reproof into words, but at the same time we assume an expression suitable to the occasion! To do this effectively, however, a certain amount of discretion is required, or we run the risk of appearing ridiculous. It is the same with regard to eurythmy. Movements of a type approaching dancing or mime when added to the essential eurythmy movements are in danger of appearing grotesque and, if applied in an exaggerated manner, given an appearance of crudity, even of vulgarity. On the other hand, pure eurythmy movements are the truest means of giving outward and visible expression to all that is contained in the human soul.

That is the essential point—that eurythmy is visible speech, visible music. One can go even further and maintain that the movements of eurythmy do actually proceed out of the inner organization of the human being. A person who says, 'As far as I am concerned, speech and music are all-sufficient; there can surely be no need to extend the sphere of art; I, for my part, have not the slightest wish for eurythmy,' is, of course, perfectly right from his particular point of view. There is always a certain justification for any opinion, however conventional or pedantic. Why should one not hold such opinions? There is certainly no reason why one should not — none at all; but it cannot be said that such a standpoint shows any really deep artistic feeling and understanding. A truly artistic nature welcomes everything that could possibly serve to widen and enrich the whole field of art.

The materials used in sculpture — bronze, clay and marble — already exist in nature and yield themselves up to the sculptor as the medium of his artistic expression; this is also true of colour in the case of the painter. When, however, in addition to all this, the movements of eurythmy, drawn forth as they have been from the very well-spring of nature and developed according to its laws, when such movements arise as a means of artistic expression, then enthusiasm burns in the soul of the true artist at the prospect of the whole sphere of art being thus widened and enriched.

A great deal can be learned about the individual eurythmy movements from a study of the models or wooden figures that illustrate the fundamental eurythmy gestures. Here it is only possible to give some indication of what underlies these wooden figures, and of all that can be revealed by them with regard to the nature and character of the various movements. These models are intended to represent the fundamental laws of eurythmy which are carried over into the actual movements themselves. Every eurythmy movement may be looked upon as being of a threefold nature; and it is this threefold aspect which is embodied in the models. In the first place there is the movement as such; then there is the feeling that lies within the movement; and lastly there is the character that flows out of the soul life and streams into the movement.

It must, however, be understood that these wooden models have been designed in a quite unusual manner. They are in no way intended to be plastic representations of the human form. This comes more within the sphere of the sculptor and the painter. The models are intended to portray the laws of eurythmy as these are expressed through the human body. In designing them, the point was not in any way to reproduce the human figure in beautiful, plastic form. And in witnessing a eurythmy demonstration, anyone who would regard beauty of face as an essential attribute of a eurythmist is labouring under a delusion as to the nature of eurythmy. Whether the eurythmist is beautiful or not beautiful, young or old, is a matter of no consequence. The whole point is whether or not the inmost nature of the eurythmist is carried over into, and expressed through, the plastic form of the movements.

Now if we look at the eurythmy model for H, for instance, the question might naturally arise: 'In what direction is the face turned? Do the eyes look upwards or straight ahead?' But that is not the first thing to be considered. In the first place we have, embodied in the model as a whole, the movement as such; that is to say, the arm movements or the movements of the legs. Secondly, in the draping of the veil, in the way the veil is held, drawn close to the body, or thrown into the air, or allowed to fall again or to fly out in waves—all this gives the opportunity for adding to the more intellectual expression of the soul life as shown through the movement another quality of the soul life, that of feeling.

At the back of the models there is always an indication of what the different colours are intended to represent. In the case of all the models certain places are marked with a third colour, and this is intended to show where the eurythmist, in carrying out the particular movement, should feel a definite tension of the muscles. This tension can be shown in any part of the body. It may have to be felt in the forehead, for instance, or in the nape of the neck, while in other places the muscles should be left in a state of complete relaxation. The eurythmist experiences the movements quite differently according to whether they are carried out with relaxed muscles or with the muscles in a state of tension; whether the arm is stretched out more or less passively or whether there is a conscious tension in the muscles of the arm and hand; whether, when bending, the muscles that are brought into play are stretched and tense or whether the bending movement leaves the muscles comparatively inactive. Through this consciously experienced tension of the muscles, character is brought into the movement.

In other words, there lies in the whole way in which the movement as such is formed something which might be described as being the expression of the human soul as manifested through visible speech. The actual spoken words, however, also have nuances of their own, their own special shades of feeling. For instance, fear may be expressed in a sentence, or joy, or delight. All these things can be shown by the eurythmist in the way in which he or she carries out the movements. The manipulation of the veil—the way in which it floats, the way in which it is allowed to fall—all this provides a means whereby these feelings can be brought to expression in eurythmy. So we see how the movement, when accompanied by the use of the veil, becomes permeated with feeling, and how, when there is added a conscious tension of the muscles, the movement acquires character as well as feeling. If the eurythmist is able to experience this tension or relaxation of the muscles in the right way, a corresponding experience will be transmitted to the onlooker, who will himself feel all that lies in the visible speech of eurythmy as character, feeling and movement.

The whole artistic conception of these models, both as regards their construction and their colouring, is based on the idea of separating the purely eurythmy element in the human being from those elements which are not so definitely connected with eurythmy. The moment a eurythmist becomes conscious of possessing a charming face, in that moment something is introduced into eurythmy that is completely foreign to its nature; on the other hand, the knowledge of how to make conscious use of the muscles of the face does form an essential part of eurythmy. For this reason, the fact that many people prefer to see a beautiful eurythmist on the stage, rather than one who is less beautiful, shows a lack of true artistic judgement. The outward appearance of a human being when not engaged in eurythmy should not in any way be taken into consideration.

These models, then, have been designed in such a way that they portray the human being only in so far as he reveals himself through the movements of eurythmy.

It would indeed be a good thing if, in the whole development of art, this principle were to be more generally adopted — I mean the principle of putting on one side everything that does not definitely belong to the sphere of the art in question, everything that cannot be expressed through the medium of this art and that does not strictly come within the range of its possibilities. A distinction should always be made — particularly when dealing with an art such as eurythmy, which reveals so directly, so truly and so sincerely the life of the human being in its threefold aspect of body, soul and spirit — between what can legitimately be revealed through the medium of any particular art and what does not lie within its true scope.

Whenever I have been asked: 'Up to what age can one do eurythmy?', my answer has always been: 'There is no age limit.' Eurythmy can be started at the age of 3 and can be continued up to the age of 90. The personality can find expression through eurythmy at each and every period of life, and through eurythmy the beauty of both youth and age can be revealed.

All that I have said up to this point has reference to eurythmy purely as an art, and, indeed, it was along purely artistic lines that eurythmy was developed in the first instance. When eurythmy was inaugurated in 1912, there was no thought of its developing along any but artistic lines, no thought of bringing it before the world in any other form.

But shortly after the founding of the Waldorf school it was discovered that eurythmy can serve as a very important tool of education; and we are now in a position to recognize the full significance of eurythmy from the educational point of view. In the Waldorf school, eurythmy has been made a compulsory subject both for boys and girls, right through the school, from the lowest to the highest class; and it has become apparent that what is thus brought to the children as visible speech and music is accepted and absorbed by them in just as natural a way as they absorb spoken language or song in their very early years. The child feels his way quite naturally into the movements of eurythmy. And, indeed, in comparison with eurythmy, the other forms of gymnastics have shown themselves to be of a somewhat one-sided nature. For these other kinds of gymnastics bear within them to some extent the materialistic attitude of mind so prevalent in our day. And for this reason they take as their starting point the physical body. Eurythmy takes the physical body into consideration also, but in the case of eurythmy body, soul and spirit work harmoniously together so that here we are dealing with an ensouled and spiritualized form of gymnastics. The child feels this. He feels that each movement that he makes does not arise merely in response to a physical necessity, but that every one of his movements is permeated with a soul and spiritual element, which streams through the arms and, indeed, through the whole body. The child absorbs eurythmy into the very depths of his being. The Waldorf school has already been in existence for some years, and the experience lying behind us justified us in saying that in this school unusual attention is paid to the cultivation of initiative, of will—qualities sorely needed by humanity in the present day. This initiative of the will is developed quite remarkably through eurythmy, when, as in the Waldorf school, it is used as a means of education. One thing, however, must be made perfectly clear, and that is that the greatest possible misunderstanding would arise if for one moment it were to be imagined that eurythmy could be taught in the schools and looked upon as a valuable asset in education if, at the same time, as an art it were to be neglected and underestimated. Eurythmy must in the first place be looked upon as an art, and in this it differs in no respect from the other arts. And in the same way that the other arts are taught in the schools, but have an independent artistic existence of their own in the world, so eurythmy also can only be taught in the schools when it is fully recognized as an art and given its proper place within our modern civilization.

Shortly after the founding of the Waldorf school, a number of doctors found their way into the anthroposophical movement and started to practise on the basis of an anthroposophical perspective. These doctors expressed the urgent wish that the movements of eurythmy—drawn out of the healthy nature of the human being and offering to the human being a means of expression suited to his whole organization—should be adapted where necessary, and placed at the service of the art of healing. Eurythmy from its very nature is forever seeking an outlet through the human being. Anyone who understands the hand, for example, must be aware that it was not formed merely to lie still and be looked at. The fingers are quite meaningless when they are inactive. They only acquire significance when they seize things, grasp them, when their passivity is transformed into movement. Their very form reveals the movement inherent within them. The same may be said of the human being as a whole. What we know under the name of eurythmy is nothing else than the means whereby the human organism can find a healthy outlet through movement. So that certain of the movements of eurythmy, though naturally differing somewhat from the movements that we use in eurythmy as an art, and having undergone a certain metamorphosis, can be made use of and developed into eurythmy therapy. Such eurythmy therapy can be of extreme value in the treatment of illness and can be applied in those cases where one knows the way in which a certain movement will react upon a certain organ with beneficial results.

In this domain also we have had good results among the children of the Waldorf school. But it is of course necessary that we should possess a true insight into the nature of the child. For instance, a child may have certain weaknesses and be generally in a delicate state of health. Such a child is then given those particular movements likely to assist in the re-establishment of his health. And along these lines we have indeed had the most brilliant results. But this, as also the educational side of eurythmy, is entirely dependent on the successful development of eurythmy as an art.

It must frankly be admitted that eurythmy is still at a very early stage of its development. A beginning, however, has certainly been made and we are striving to make it ever more perfect. There was a time, for instance, when we had not as yet introduced the silent, unaccompanied movement of the eurythmist at the beginning and end of a poem. Such movement is intended to convey in the first instance an introductory impression and, in the second, an impression reminiscent of the content of the poem. At that time also there were no lighting effects. Lighting in various tones and colours has not been introduced with a view to illustrating or intensifying any particular situation but is in itself actually of a eurythmy nature. The point is not that certain effects of light should correspond with what is taking place on the stage at a given moment, but the whole system of lighting, as this has been developed in eurythmy, consists of the interplay between one lighting effect and another. Thus there arises a complete system of eurythmy lighting which bears within it the same character and the same shades of feeling as are being simultaneously expressed on the stage in another way through the movements of the eurythmists, or the eurythmist, as the case may be.

And so, as eurythmy develops and attains ever greater perfection, very much more will have to be added to the whole picture of eurythmy as this is presented on the stage, very much will have to be added to all that we can now see when witnessing a eurythmy demonstration.

I could indeed speak about eurythmy the whole night through, carrying on this lecture without a break into the lecture of tomorrow morning. I am afraid, however, that my audience would hardly benefit by such a proceeding, and the same certainly applies to any eurythmists who may be present! The great thing is that all I have said today in this introductory lecture will be realized in practice for you tomorrow, when you witness the performance; after all, where art is concerned, a practical demonstration is of more value than any lecture.

The essentials of education

What are we doing in eurythmy? We divide it into tone eurythmy and speech eurythmy. In tone eurythmy we produce in the child movements that correspond to the form of the astral body, in speech eurythmy movements that correspond to the ego organization. We are thereby working consciously on the development of the soul by bringing the physical elements into play in tone eurythmy; we are working consciously on the development of the spirit by bringing the corresponding physical elements into play in speech eurythmy. Such activity, however, can only proceed from a complete understanding of the human organization. Those who imagine they can gain access to the being of a person through external physiology and experimental psychology, which is really nothing other than a kind of external physiology, would similarly fail to realize that when they want to produce a given mood in a person they must not beat on a wooden tray but make music. In the same way, knowledge must not remain at a standstill with abstract, logical rules but rise to a conception of human life that does not only comprise dead nature, or life that has died or is conceived of in a dead way. When we rise from abstract principles to the sculptural formative elements and perceive how every natural law moulds itself sculpturally, we learn to know the etheric body of the human being. When we begin to hear in an inner, spiritual sense how the cosmic rhythm is expressing itself in that most wonderful musical instrument which the astral body makes of the human being, we learn to know the astral nature of the human being. What we must be conscious of may be expressed as follows. First lesson: we learn to know the physical body of the human being in an abstract, logical sense. Then we turn to the sculptural formative activity with intuitive cognition and we learn to know the etheric body. Third lesson: as physiologists we become musicians and look at the human being as we look at a musical instrument, at an organ or a violin in which we see music realized. Thus we learn to know the astral human being. And when we learn to know the genius of speech as it works creatively in the words, not merely connecting it with words through the external memory, we gain knowledge of the ego organization of the human being.

The inner nature of music — tone eurythmy

Though they are quite fragmentary and incomplete and must be elaborated further at the next opportunity, I wish to emphasize again that yesterday's lecture and today's are intended to give teachers in school what they need as background for their instruction.

Yesterday, I spoke on the one hand of the role that the interval of the fifth plays in musical experience and on the other hand of the roles played by the third and the seventh. You have been able to gather from this account that music progressing in fifths is still connected with a musical experience in which the human being is actually brought out of himself; with the feeling for the fifth, a person actually feels transported. This becomes more obvious if we take the scales through the range of seven octaves — from the contra-tones up to the tones above c — and consider that it is possible for the fifth to occur twelve times within these seven scales. In the sequence of the seven musical scales, we discover hidden, as it were, an additional twelve-part scale with the interval of the fifth.

What does this really mean in relation to the whole musical experience? It means that within the experience of the fifth the human being with his 'I' is in motion outside his physical organization. He paces the seven scales in twelve steps, as it were. He is therefore in motion outside his physical organization through the experience of the fifth.

Returning to the experience of the third—in both the major and minor third—we arrive at an inner motion of the human being. The 'I' is, so to speak, within the confines of the human organism; the human being experiences the interval of the third inwardly. In the transition from a third to a fifth—though there is much in between with which we are not concerned here—the human being in fact experiences the transition from inner to outer experience. One therefore can say that in the case of the experience of the third the mood is one of consolidation of the inner being, of a person becoming aware of the human being within himself. The experience of the fifth brings awareness of the human being within the divine world order. The experience of the fifth is of an expansion into the vast universe, while the experience of the third is a return of the human being into the structure of his own organization. In between lies the experience of the fourth.

The experience of the fourth is perhaps one of the most interesting for anyone who wishes to penetrate the secrets of the musical element. This is not because the experience of the fourth in itself is the most interesting but because it arises at the dividing line between the experience of the fifth of the outer world and the experience of the third in the human being's inner being. The experience of the fourth lies right at the border of the human organism. The human being, however, senses not the outer world but the spiritual world in the fourth. He beholds himself from outside (to borrow an expression referring to vision for an experience that has to do with hearing). Though the human being is not conscious of it, the sensation he experiences with the fourth is based on the feeling that the human being himself is among the gods. While he has forgotten his own self in the experience of the fifth in order to be among the gods, in the experience of the fourth he need not forget his own being in order to be among the gods. With the experience of the fourth, the human being moves about in the divine world; he stands precisely at the border of his humanness, retaining it, yet viewing it from the other side.

The experience of the fifth as a spiritual experience was the first to be lost to humanity. The modern human being no longer has the experience of the fifth that still existed, let us say, four to five hundred years before our era. At that time the human being truly felt in the experience of the fifth 'I stand within the spiritual world'. He required no instrument in order to produce outwardly the interval of a fifth. Because he still possessed imaginative consciousness, he felt that the fifth, which he himself had produced, took its course in the divine realm. The human being still had imaginations in the musical element. There was still an objectivity, a musical objectivity, in the experience of the fifth. The human being lost this earlier than the objective experience of the fourth. The experience of the fourth, much later on, was such that during this experience the human being believed that he lived in and interacted with something etheric. With the experience of the fourth he felt — if I may say so — the holy wind that had placed him into the physical world. Based on what they said, it is possible that Ambrose[30] and Augustine[31] still felt this. Then this experience of the fourth was also lost. An outer instrument was required in order to be objectively certain of the fourth.

We thus have pointed out at the same time what the musical experience was like in very ancient ages of human evolution. Human beings did not yet know the third; they descended only to the fourth. They did not distinguish between 'I sing' and 'There is singing'. These two were one for them. They were outside themselves when they sang and at the same time had an outer instrument. They had an impression, an imagination of a wind instrument or of a string instrument. Musical instruments appeared to human beings at first as imaginations. Musical instruments were not invented through experimentation; with the exception of the piano they have been derived from the spiritual world.

With this, we have described the origin of song as well. It is hard today to give an idea of what song itself was like in the age when the experience of the fifth was still pure. Song was indeed something akin to an expression of the word. People sang, but this was at the same time a speaking of the spiritual world. People were conscious that if they spoke of cherries and grapes they used earthly words; if they spoke of the gods, they had to sing.

Then came the time when human beings no longer had imaginations. They still retained the remnants of imaginations, however, though they are not recognized as such today—they are the words of language. The spiritual element incarnated into the tones of song, which in turn incarnated into the elements of words. This was a step into the physical world. The inner emancipation of the song element into arias and the like took place after that; this was a later development.

If we return to the primeval song of humanity, we find that it was a speaking about the gods and the deeds of the gods. As I mentioned earlier, the fact of the twelve fifths in the seven scales is evidence that the possibility of motion outside the human realm existed in music in the interval of the fifth. Only with the fourth does the human being really approach himself with the musical element.

Yesterday, someone said quite rightly that the human being senses an emptiness in the interval of the fifth. Naturally, he must experience something empty in the fifth, since he no longer has imaginations, and the fifth corresponds to an imagination while the third corresponds to a perception within a person's being. Today, therefore, the human being feels an emptiness in the fifth and must fill it with the substantiality of the instrument. This is the transition of the musical element from the more spiritual age to the later materialistic age.

For earlier ages, the relationship between the musical human being and his instrument must be pictured as the greatest possible unity. In Greece, actors even felt the need to amplify their voices with an instrument. The process of drawing the musical experience inward came later. Previously, the human being felt that in relation to music he carried a certain circle of tones within himself that reached downward, excluding the realm of tones below the contra C. Upward, it did not reach the tones beyond C but was a closed circle. The human being then had the awareness, 'I have been given a small circle of the musical element. Out there in the cosmos the musical element continues in both directions. I need the instruments in order to reach this cosmic musical element.'

Now we must take the other aspects of music into consideration if we wish to become acquainted with this whole matter. The focus of music today is harmony. I am referring to music as a whole, not song or instrumental music. The element of harmony takes hold directly of human feeling. What is expressed in harmonies is experienced by human feeling. Now, feeling is actually the centre of human experience as a whole. On one side, feeling passes over into willing, on the other side, feeling passes into thinking. In looking at the human being, we can say that feeling is in the middle, passing into thinking on the one hand and into willing on the other. Harmony directly addresses itself to feeling and is experienced in it. The whole emotional nature of the human being, however, is actually twofold. We have a feeling that is more inclined to thinking—when we feel our thoughts, for instance—and we have a feeling more inclined to willing. When we engage in an action we feel whether it pleases or displeases us in the same way we feel pleasure or displeasure with an idea. Feeling is actually divided into these two realms.

The peculiar thing about the musical element is that it should not penetrate completely into thinking—because it would cease to be something musical the moment it was taken hold of by the brain's conceptual faculty—nor should it sink down completely into the sphere of willing. We cannot imagine, for example, that the musical element itself could become a direct will impulse without being an abstract sign. When you hear the ringing of the dinner bell, you will go because it announces that it is time to go to dinner, but you will not take the bell's musical element as the impulse for the will. This illustrates that music should not reach into the realm of willing any more than into that of thinking. It must be contained in both directions. The musical experience must take place within the realm situated between thinking and willing. It must unfold in that part of the human being that does not belong to ordinary daytime consciousness but has something to do with that which comes down from spiritual worlds, incarnates, and then passes again through death. It is present in the subconscious. For this reason, music has no direct equivalent in outer nature. In adapting himself to the earth, the human being finds his way into what can be grasped conceptually and what he wills to do. Music, however, does not extend this far into thinking and willing, yet the element of harmony has a tendency to stream towards thinking. It must not penetrate thinking but it streams towards it. This streaming into the region of our spirit where we otherwise think is brought about by the harmony of the melody.

The element of melody guides the musical element from the realm of feeling up to that of thinking. You do not find what is contained in thinking in the thematic melody, but the theme does contain the element that reaches up into the same realm where mental images are otherwise formed. Melody contains something akin to mental images, but it is not a mental image; it clearly takes its course in the life of feeling. It tends upwards, however, so that the feeling is experienced in the human head. The significance of the element of melody in human nature is that it makes the head of the human being accessible to feelings. Otherwise, the head only deals with concepts. Through melody the head becomes open to feeling, to actual feeling. It is as if you brought the heart into the head through melody. In the melody you become free, as you normally are in thinking; feeling becomes serene and purified. All outer aspects are eliminated from it, but at the same time it remains feeling through and through.

Just as harmony can tend upwards towards thinking, so it can tend downwards towards willing. It must not penetrate the realm of willing, however; it must restrain itself, as it were, and this is accomplished through rhythm. Melody thus carries harmony upwards; rhythm carries harmony in the direction of willing. This is restricted willing, a measured will that runs its course in time; it does not proceed outwards but remains bound to the human being himself. It is genuine feeling that extends into the realm of willing.

Now it becomes understandable that when a child first enters school it comprehends melodies more readily than harmonies. Of course, one must not take this pedantically; pedantry must never play a role in the artistic. It goes without saying that one can introduce the child to all sorts of things. Just as the child should comprehend only fifths during the first years of school—at most also fourths, but not thirds; it begins to grasp thirds inwardly only from age 9 onwards—one can also say that the child easily understands the element of melody, but it begins to understand the element of harmony only when it reaches the age of 9 or 10. Naturally, the child already understands the tone, but the actual element of harmony can be cultivated in the child only after the above age has been reached. The rhythmic element, on the other hand, assumes the greatest variety of forms. The child will comprehend a certain inner rhythm while it is still very young. Aside from this instinctively experienced rhythm, however, the child should not be troubled until after it is 9 years old with the rhythm that is experienced, for example, in the elements of instrumental music. Only then should the child's attention be called to these things. In the sphere of music, too, the age levels can indicate what needs to be done. These age levels are approximately the same as those found elsewhere in Waldorf education.

Taking a closer look at rhythm, we see that since the rhythmic element is related to the nature of will—the human being must inwardly activate his will when he wishes to experience music — it is the rhythmic element that kindles music in the first place. Regardless of the human being's relationship to rhythm, all rhythm is based on the mysterious connection between pulse and breath, the ratio of 18 breaths per minute to an average of 72 pulse beats per minute. This ratio of 1:4 naturally can be modified in any number of ways; it can also be individualized. Each person has his own experience regarding rhythm; since these experiences are approximately the same, however, people understand each other in reference to rhythm. All rhythmic experience bases itself on the mysterious relationship between breathing and the heartbeat, the circulation of the blood. We can thus say that while the melody is carried from the heart to the head on the flow of the breath — and therefore in an outer slackening and inner creation of quality — the rhythm is carried on the waves of the blood circulation from the heart to the limbs, and in the limbs it is arrested as will. From this you can see how the musical element really pervades the whole human being.

Picture the whole human being experiencing the musical element as a human spirit: the ability to experience the element of melody gives you the head of this spirit. The ability to experience the element of harmony gives you the chest, the central organ of the spirit; and the ability to experience rhythm gives you the limbs of the spirit. What have I described for you here? I have described the human etheric body. If you depict only the whole musical experience, and if you do this correctly, you actually have before you the human etheric body. It is just that instead of 'head' we say 'melody'; instead of 'rhythmic human being' — because it is lifted upward — we say 'harmony'; and instead of 'limb human being' — we cannot say here 'metabolic human being' — we say 'rhythm'. We have the entire human being etherically before us. The musical experience is nothing other than this. The human being experiences himself as an etheric body in the experience of the fourth, as a kind of summation of forms within him. The experience of the fourth contains a touch of melody, a touch of harmony, a touch of rhythm, but all interwoven in such a way that they are no longer distinguishable. The entire human being is experienced spiritually at the threshold in the experience of the fourth: we experience the etheric human being.

If music today were not a part of the materialistic age, if all that the human being experiences today did not contaminate the musical element, then what a person possesses today in terms of music, which itself has reached an advanced stage in world history, would make him a natural anthroposophist. If you wish to experience the musical element consciously, you cannot but experience it anthroposophically.

If you take these things as they are, you can ponder, for example, over the following point. Everywhere in ancient traditions of spiritual life mention is made of the human being's sevenfold nature. The theosophical movement also adopted this view of the sevenfold nature of the human being. When I wrote my *Theosophy*, I had to speak of a ninefold human being, further dividing the three individual elements. I arrived at the sevenfold from a ninefold organization.

9 (Spirit Man)
8 (Life Spirit)
7 (Spirit Self)   6 (consciousness soul)
                                   5 (intellectual soul)
3 (astral or sentient body)   4 (sentient soul)
2 (etheric body)
1 (physical body)

Since three and four overlap, as do six and seven, I too arrived at the sevenfold human being in *Theosophy*. This book, however, could never have been written in the age dominated by the experience of the fifth. The reason is that in that age all spiritual experience was based on the awareness that the number of planets was contained in the seven scales, and the number of signs in the zodiac was contained in the twelve fifths within the seven scales. The great mystery of the human being was revealed in the circle of fifths, and in that period you could not write about theosophy in any way but by arriving at the sevenfold human being. My *Theosophy* was written in an age during which the third is predominantly experienced by human beings, in other words, in the age of introversion. One must seek the spiritual in a similar way, descending from the interval of the fifth by division to the interval of the third. I therefore also had to divide the individual elements of the human being. You can say that those other books that speak of the sevenfold human being stem from the tradition of the age of the fifth, from the tradition of the circle of fifths. My *Theosophy*[32] stems from the age in which the third plays the dominant musical role and in which, because of this, the more complex situation arises that the more inward element tends towards the minor side, the more outward element towards the major side. This causes the indistinct overlapping between the sentient body and sentient soul. The sentient soul relates to the minor third, the sentient body to the major third. The facts of human evolution are expressed in musical development more clearly than anywhere else. But as I already told you yesterday, one must abandon concepts; abstract conceptualizing will get you nowhere here.

Acoustics, or tone physiology, has nothing to contribute. Acoustics has no significance except in physics. A tone physiology that would have significance for music itself does not exist. If one wishes to comprehend the musical element, one must enter into the spiritual aspect.

You see how the interval of the fourth is situated between the fifth and the third. The human being feels transported in the fifth; in the third he feels himself within himself; in the fourth he is on the border between himself and the world. Yesterday I told you that the seventh was the dominant interval for the Atlanteans.[33] They only had intervals of the seventh, though they did not have the same feeling as we have today. When they made music they were transported completely beyond themselves; they were within the great, all-pervading spirituality of the universe in an absolute motion. They were being moved. This motion was still contained in the experience of the fifth as well. Again, the sixth is in between. From this we realize that the human being experiences these three steps, the seventh, the sixth and the fifth, in a transported condition; he enters into his own being in the fourth; he dwells within himself in the third. Only in the future will the human being experience the octave's full musical significance. He has not yet reached an assured experience of the second; these are matters that lie in the future. When the human being's inner life intensifies, he will experience the second, and finally he will be sensitive to the single tone. I do not know whether some of you will recall that I once said during a question-and-answer session in Dornach that the single tone will be experienced as something that is musically differentiated, that already musical differentiation resides within the single tone.

If you focus on what is said here, you will grasp better the forms[34] that appear in tone eurythmy. You will also grasp something else. You will, for example, understand the reason why an instinctive feeling arises to interpret the lower segments of the octave—the prime, second and third—by backward movements and the upper tones—the fifth, sixth and seventh—by forward movements.

These are more or less the shapes that can be used as typical forms. In the case of the forms that have been developed for individual musical compositions, you will be able to sense that these forms express the experience of the fourth or the fifth.

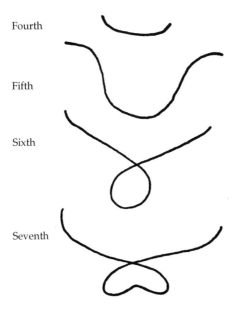

Fourth

Fifth

Sixth

Seventh

In eurythmy it is necessary that this part here—the descent of harmony through rhythm into willing—finds emphatic expression in form. The individual intervals are contained in the forms as such, executed by the eurythmist. Then, however, what passes from the inter-

vals into rhythm must be experienced fully by the performer in these forms; and quite by itself the instinct will
arise to make as small a movement as possible with the
fourth without standing still. You see, the fourth in fact
represents real perception, but perception from the other
side. It is as if the eye, in perceiving itself, looks back on
itself; this, then, is the experience of the fourth gained
from the soul.

The interval of the fifth is a real experience of Imagination. The person who can experience fifths correctly is
actually in a position to know on the subjective level what
Imagination is like. Anyone who experiences sixths knows
what Inspiration is. Finally, the person who fully experiences sevenths—if he survives the experience—knows
what Intuition is. What I mean is that in the experience of
the seventh the composition of the soul is the same as
occurs during clairvoyance with regard to Intuition. The
composition of the soul during the experience of the sixth
is that of Inspiration during clairvoyance. The experience
of the fifth is a real imaginative experience. In clairvoyance, such composition of soul simply has vision added.
Such composition of soul is definitely present in the case
of music.

This is why you hear everywhere that in the older
mystery schools and remaining mystery traditions clairvoyant cognition is also called a musical cognition, a
spiritual-musical cognition. Though people today no
longer know why, the mysteries refer to the existence of
two kinds of cognition, ordinary physical, intellectual

cognition and spiritual cognition, which is in fact a musical cognition, a cognition living in the musical element. It would not actually be so difficult to popularize the understanding of the threefold human being if only people today were conscious of their musical experiences. Certainly to some extent people do have sensitivity for music, but, as human beings, they are not really within the experience of the musical element. They actually stand alongside it. The experience of the musical element is as yet quite limited. If it were really to become alive in the human being, he would feel: my etheric head is in the element of melody, and the physical has fallen away. Here, I have one aspect of the human organization. The element of harmony contains the centre of my etheric system; again, the physical has fallen away. Then we reach the next octave, again in the limb system—it is obvious and goes without saying—I find the element that appears as the rhythmic element of music.

What, then, has been the musical evolution of the human being? It begins with the experience of the spiritual, the actual presence of the spiritual in tone, in the musical tone structure. The spiritual fades away; the human being retains the tone structure. Later, he links it with the word, which is a remnant of the spiritual; and what he had earlier as imaginations, namely, the instruments, he fashions here in the physical world out of physical substance as his musical instruments. To the extent that they arouse the musical mood, the instruments are all derived from the spiritual world. When he built physical musical instruments, the human being simply filled the empty spaces that remained after he no longer beheld the spiritual. Into those spaces he put the physical instruments.

It is correct to say that in music more than anywhere else one can see how the transition to the materialistic age proceeds. In the place where musical instruments resound today, spiritual entities stood formerly. They are gone, they have disappeared from the ancient clairvoyance. If the human being wishes to take objective hold of the musical element, however, he needs something that does not exist in outer nature. Outer nature offers him no equivalent to the musical element; therefore he requires musical instruments.

The musical instruments basically are a clear reflection of the fact that music is experienced by the whole human being. The wind instruments prove that the head of the human being experiences music. The string instruments are living proof that music is experienced in the chest, primarily expressed in the arms. All percussion instruments — or those in between string and percussion instruments — are evidence of how the musical element is expressed in the third part of the human being's nature, the limb system. Also, everything connected with the wind instruments has a more intimate relation to the element of melody than that which is connected with the string instruments, which have a relation to the element of harmony. That which is connected with percussion possesses more inner rhythm and relates to the rhythmic element. An orchestra is an image of the human being; it must not include a piano, however. Why is that? The musical instruments are derived from the spiritual world; the piano, however, in which the tones are abstractly lined up next to each other, is created only in the physical world by people. All instruments like the flute or violin originate musically from the higher world. A piano is like the philistine who no longer contains within him the higher human being. The piano is the philistine instrument. It is fortunate that there is such an instrument, or else the philistine would have no music at all. The piano arises out of a materialistic experience of music. It is therefore the instrument that can be used most conveniently to evoke the musical element within the material realm. Pure matter was put to use so that the piano could become an expression of the musical element. Naturally, the piano is a beneficial instrument—otherwise we would have to rely from the beginning on the spiritual in musical instruction in our materialistic age—but it is the one instrument that actually, in a musical sense, must be overcome. The human being must get away from the impressions of the piano if he wishes to experience the actual musical element.

It is therefore always a great experience when a composition by an artist who basically lives completely in the element of music, such as Bruckner,[35] is played on the piano. In Bruckner's composition the piano seems to disappear from the room! One forgets the piano and thinks that one is hearing other instruments; this is indeed so in

Bruckner's case. It proves that something of the essentially spiritual, which lies at the basis of all music, still lived in Bruckner, though in a very instinctive way.

These are the things that I wished to tell you today, though in a fragmentary, informal way. I believe we will soon have an opportunity to continue with these matters. Then I shall go into more detail concerning various aspects.

Eurythmy as visible speech

These lectures dealing with the nature of eurythmy are in response to a request from Frau Dr Steiner, who believes it to be necessary in order to lay the foundation of an exact eurythmy tradition, to recapitulate in the first place all that has been given in the domain of speech eurythmy at different times to different people. To this repetition fresh material will be added in order to widen the field of eurythmy expression. Such material will, however, not be set apart in separate chapters, but will be given in connection with each individual point as this comes under discussion.

I shall endeavour to deal with eurythmy from its various aspects; not only from the artistic side, which naturally calls for our first consideration here, but also from the point of view of education and healing.

The first lecture will be in the nature of an introduction and this will be followed by a lecture dealing with the first elements of speech eurythmy. In every branch of eurythmy activity it is necessary above all that the personality, the whole human being of the eurythmist should be brought into play, so that eurythmy may become an expression of life itself. This cannot be achieved unless one enters into the spirit of eurythmy, feeling it actually as visible speech. As in the case of all artistic appreciation, it is quite possible for anyone to enjoy eurythmy as a spectator, without having acquired any knowledge of its essential basis, just as it is quite unnecessary to have studied harmony or counterpoint to be able to appreciate music. For it is an accepted fact of human evolution that the healthily developed human being carries within him a natural appreciation and understanding of art.

Art must work through its own inherent power. Art must be self-evident. Those, however, who are studying eurythmy, whose duty it is in some way or another to bring eurythmy before the world, must penetrate into the actual essence and nature of eurythmy in just the same way as, let us say, the musician, the painter or the sculptor must enter into the nature of his own particular art. If we wish to enter into the true nature of eurythmy we must of necessity enter into the true nature of the human being. For eurythmy, to a far greater extent than any other art, makes use of what lies in the nature of the human being himself. Take for example various other arts, arts which need instruments or tools for their expression. You find no instrument or tool so nearly akin to the human being as the instrument made use of by the eurythmist. The art of mime and the art of dancing do indeed to some extent make use of the human being as a means of artistic expression. With the art of mime, however, that which is expressed through the mime itself is merely subordinate to the performance as a whole, for such a performance does not depend entirely upon the artistic, sculptural use of the human being. In such a case this same human being is made use of in order to imitate something that is already present in the human being here on earth.

Furthermore, in the case of the art of mime we find as a rule that the gestures are used mainly to emphasize and render clearer something which is made use of by people in everyday life; that is to say, mime emphasizes speech. In order to bring a more intimate note into speech, gesture is added. Thus we are here concerned with something which merely adds in some small measure to the scope of that which is already present in the human being on the physical plane.

In the art of dancing—if we may use the word 'art' in such a context when dancing rises to the level of art—we are dealing with an outpouring of the emotions, of the will, into movements of the human body, whereby only those possibilities of movement are developed further which are inherent in the human being and already present elsewhere on the physical plane. In eurythmy we are dealing with something that can be found nowhere in the human being in ordinary physical life, but which is a creation coming from the spiritual worlds through and through. We are dealing with something which makes use of the human being, which makes use of the human form and its movement as a means of expression.

Now the question arises: what is really expressed in eurythmy? This you will only understand when you begin to realize that eurythmy is actually visible speech. With regard to speech itself the following must be said. When we give form to speech by means of mime, ordinary speech itself provides us with a picture, with an image; when, however, we give form to speech itself, to sound as such, we find that the latter contains within it no such image. Speech arises as a separate, independent product from out of the human being himself. Nowhere in nature do we find that which reveals itself in speech, that which comes into being through speech.

For this reason eurythmy must, by its very nature, be something that represents a primal creation. Speech — let us take this as our starting point — speech appears as a product of the human larynx and of those organs of speech which are in some way connected with it. What is the nature of the larynx? This question must eventually be raised, for I have often shown how in eurythmy the whole human being must become a sort of larynx. We must therefore ask ourselves the question: of what significance is the larynx? Now if you look upon speech merely as a production of the larynx, you will gain no conception of what is really proceeding from it, of what is being fashioned within it. Here it would perhaps be well to remind ourselves of a remarkable tradition which today is little understood, and of which you find some indication when you take the beginning of St John's Gospel: 'In the Beginning was the Word, and the Word was with God, and a God was the Word.' The Word. Of course that which we today imagine to be the Word is something which does not make the slightest sense in relation to the opening sentences of this Gospel. Nevertheless they are continually quoted. People believe they can make sense of them. They do not, however, succeed. For it is an undeniable fact that the concept of the word as understood by the human being of today is often truly expressed by his saying something of this kind: what is a name but mere sound and smoke, mist and vapour? In a certain sense he values the word itself little in comparison with its underlying concept. He feels a certain superiority in thus being able to value the word little in comparison with the thought. When, therefore, one puts oneself in the position of the human being of today and considers what he understands by the term word, the beginning of St John's Gospel has indeed no meaning. For consider: the Word? We have so many words: which word? It can only be a definite, concrete word. And what is the nature of this Word? That is the question.

Now behind the tradition that is indicated in the beginning of this Gospel lies the fact that the human being once had an instinctive knowledge of the true nature of the Word. Today, however, this knowledge has been lost. To ancient human understanding, the idea, the concept, the 'Word' comprised the whole human being as an etheric creation.

All of you, as anthroposophists, know what we mean by the etheric human being. We have the physical human being and we have the etheric human being. The physical human being, as he is described today by modern physiology and anatomy, consists both outwardly and inwardly of certain forms which can be drawn. Here, however, the fact naturally fails to be taken into account that what is drawn only represents the very smallest part of the physical human being, for the physical body is at the same time fluid; it consists also of air and warmth. These constituents are naturally not included when reference is made to the human being in physiology and anatomy. Nevertheless, it is possible to gain some idea of the nature of the physical body of the human being.

We have, however, the second element of the human being, the etheric body. If we were to attempt to draw the etheric body something extraordinarily complicated would come to expression. For the etheric body can just as little be represented as something static as can lightning. It is impossible to paint lightning; for lightning is in continual movement, lightning is in continual flow. In portraying lightning one must attempt to show it in continual flow and movement. And the same holds true of the etheric body. The etheric body is in continual motion, in continual activity.

Now these movements, these gestures which are continually in movement (of which the etheric body does not consist, but out of which it continually arises and again passes away), do we find them anywhere in the world of human beings, do we come up against them anywhere? Yes, we do. This was no secret to ancient and intuitive knowledge. We have these movements — and here, my dear friends, I must ask you to take what I am saying quite literally — in the sound formations that embody the content of speech.

Now review mentally all the sounds of speech to which your larynx gives form and utterance, inasmuch as this formative principle is applied to the entire range of articulate speech. Bear in mind all the component elements which issue from the larynx for the purpose of speech. You must realize that all these elements, proceeding as they do from the larynx, really form the component parts of that which is brought to outer expression in speech. You must realize that these sound formations consist of definite movements, the origin of which lies in the structure and form of the larynx and its neighbouring organs. They proceed from the larynx.

But these movements do not of course appear simultaneously. We cannot utter all the sounds that make up the content of speech at the same moment. How then could we utter all that makes up the content of speech? We could do so — paradoxical as this may sound it is nevertheless a fact — if we were to utter one after the other all the possible sounds from *a*, *b*, *c*, down to *z*. Try to imagine this. Imagine that someone were to say the alphabet aloud, beginning with *a*, *b* and continuing as far as *z*, with only the necessary pauses for breathing. Every spoken sound describes a certain form in the air which we cannot see but the existence of which must be assumed. It is possible, indeed, to think of these forms being retained, fixed by scientific means, without actually making a physical drawing of them.

When we utter any particular word aloud, 'tree' for example, or 'sun', we produce a quite definite shape in the air.

If we were to say the whole alphabet aloud from *a* to *z*, we should produce a very complicated shape in the air. Let us ask ourselves: what really would be the result if someone were actually to do this? It would have to take place within a certain time, as you will learn in the course of these lectures. It would have to take place within a certain time, so that on reaching *z* the first sound would not have completely disintegrated, that is to say, the *a* sound must still retain its plastic form when we have reached sound *z*. If it were actually possible in this creation of air forms to pass from *a* to *z* in such a way that the *a* sound remained when the *z* sound were reached, thus creating in the air an image of the whole alphabet, what would be the result? What sort of form should we have made? We should have created the form of the human etheric body. In this way we should have reproduced the human etheric body. If you were to repeat the alphabet aloud from *a* to *z* (one would have to do this in exactly the right way; the alphabetical order of sounds in general use today is no longer quite correct, but I am speaking now of the underlying principle), the human etheric body would be present before you.

What then would really have taken place? The human etheric body is always present. Every human being bears it within himself. What do you do therefore when you speak, when you say the alphabet aloud? You sink, so to speak, into the form of your own etheric body. What happens, then, when we utter a single word, which of course does not consist of all the sounds? Let us picture to ourselves the human being as he stands before us. He consists of physical body, etheric body, astral body and ego. He speaks a word. He sinks his consciousness into his etheric body. He forms some part of the etheric body in the air as a shape, in much the same way as you, standing before a physical body, might for instance copy the form of a hand, so that the form of the hand were made visible in the air. Now the etheric body does not consist of the same forms as those which make up the physical body, but in this case it is the forms of the etheric body which are impressed into the air. When we learn to understand this properly, we gain an insight into the most wonderful metamorphosis of the human form, an insight into the evolution of the human being. For what is this etheric body? It is the vehicle of the forces of growth; it contains within it all those forces bound up with the processes of nourishment, and also those forces connected with the power of memory. All this is imparted to the airy formations when we speak.

The inner being of the human being, in so far as this is expressed in the etheric body, is impressed into the air when we speak. When we put sounds together, words arise. When we put together the whole alphabet from beginning to end, there arises a very complicated word. This word contains every possibility of word-formation. It also contains at the same time the human being in his etheric nature. Before the human being appeared on the earth as a physical being, he already existed as an etheric being. For the etheric human being underlies the physical human being. How, then, can the etheric human being be described? The etheric human being is the Word which contains within it the entire alphabet.

Thus when we speak of the formation of this primal Word, which existed from the beginning before the physical human being came into being, we find that the element that arises in connection with speech may indeed be called a birth, a birth of the whole etheric human being when the alphabet is spoken aloud. Otherwise, in the single words, it is a partial birth, a birth of fragments, of parts of the human being. Something of the being of the human being lies in every single word as it is uttered. Let us take the word 'tree' for instance. What does it mean when we say the word 'tree'? When we say the word 'tree' it means that we describe the tree as follows. We say: that which stands there in the outer world, to which we give the name 'tree', is a part of ourselves, a part of our own etheric being. Everything in the world is a part of ourselves; nothing exists which cannot be expressed through the being of the human being. Just as the human being really gives utterance to himself, and consequently to the whole universe, when he gives utterance to the whole alphabet, so when uttering single words which represent fragments of the collective Word, of the alphabet, he gives expression to something that is a part of the universe. The entire universe would be expressed if the whole alphabet were uttered from beginning to end. Parts of the universe are expressed in the single words.

There is one thing, however, about which we must be quite clear when we think over all that lies behind sound as such. Behind sound as such there lies everything that comprises the inner being of the human being. The activity manifested by the etheric body is representative of the inner experiences of the soul in terms of feelings. We must now find our way to these feelings themselves which are experienced in the human soul.

Let us take the sound *a* as a beginning. Today we learn to utter the sound *a* when we are in that unconscious dreamy condition in which we live as very small children. This experience is later buried when the child suffers harm at school as a result of receiving wrong teaching in sound and language. When we learn to speak as a child there is really present something of the great mystery of speech. It remains, however, in a state of dreamy uncon-sciousness.

When we utter the sound *a* we feel, if our instinct is at all healthy, that this sound really proceeds from our inmost being when we are in a state of wonder and amazement.

Now this wonder is of course again only a part of the human being. The human being is no abstraction. At every waking moment of his life he is something or other. One can of course allow oneself to become sluggish or stupefied, in which case one cannot be said to be anything very definite. But the human being must always be something, even when he reduces himself to a state of torpor; at every minute of the day he must be something or other. Now he is filled with wonder, now with fear or, let us say, with aggressive activity. The human being is no abstraction; every second he must be something definite. Thus there are times when the human being is a being of wonder, a being filled with amazement. The processes at work in the etheric body when the human being experiences wonder are imprinted into the air with the help of the larynx when he utters the sound *a*. When the human being utters the sound *a* he sends out of himself a part of his own being, namely, the quality of wonder. This he imprints into the air.

We know that when a physical human being appears on earth he is born under normal circumstances as a complete human being. This complete human being comes out of the womb of the mother. He is born as a physical person with a physical form. If all the sounds of the alphabet were uttered from *a* to *z* there would arise an etheric person, only this etheric person would be imprinted into the air, born from out of the human larynx and its neighbouring organs.

When a child first sees the light, a physical person has emerged from the womb and its neighbouring organs. But the larynx differs from the womb of the mother in that it is in a continual state of creation so that fragments of the human being arise in single words. And indeed, if one were to bring together all the words of a language (which even in the case of a poet with such a rich vocabulary as Shakespeare never actually occurs), the entire etheric human being as a form in the air would be produced by means of the creative larynx, but it would be a succession of births, a continuous becoming. It would be a birth continually taking place during the process of speech. Speech is always the bringing to birth of parts of the etheric human being.

The physical larynx in turn is only the external sheath of that most wonderful organ which is present in the etheric body, and which is, as it were, the womb of the Word. And here again we are confronted with a wonderful meta-morphosis. Everything that is present in the human being is a metamorphosis of certain fundamental forms. The etheric larynx and its sheath, the physical larynx, are a metamorphosis of the uterus. In speech we have to do with the creation of the human being, with the creation of the human being as an etheric being.

This mystery of speech is indicated by the connection that we find between the vocal and sexual functions, a connection clearly illustrated in the breaking of the male voice.

We are therefore dealing with a creative activity which, welling up from the depths of cosmic life, flows outwards through the medium of speech. We see revealed in a fluctuating, ever-changing form that which otherwise withdraws itself into the mysterious depths of the human organization at the moment of physical birth. Thus we gain something which is essential for us in our artistic creative activity. We gain respect, reverence, for that creative element into which we, as artists, are placed. Theoretical discussion is useless in the realm of art. We cannot do with it; it merely leads us into abstraction. In art we need something which places us with our whole human being into the cosmic being. And how could we penetrate more deeply into the cosmic being than by becoming conscious of the relation existing between speech and the genesis of the human being. Every time that a person speaks he produces out of himself some part of that which existed in primeval times, when the human being was created out of cosmic depths, out of the etheric forces, and received form as a being of air before he acquired fluid form and, later still, his solid physical form. Every time we speak we transpose ourselves into the cosmic evolution of the human being as it was in primal ages.

Let us take an example. Let us go back once more to the sound *a*, this sound which calls up within us the human being in a state of wonder. We must realize that every time the sound *a* appears in language there lies behind it the element of wonder. Let us take the word *Wasser* (water), or the word *Pfahl* (post), any word you like in which the sound *a* occurs. In every instance, when you lay stress on the sound *a* in speech, there is present in the background a feeling of wonder; the human being filled with wonder is brought to expression in this way by means of speech.

There was a time when this was well known. It was, for example, known to the Hebrew people. For what really lay behind the *a*, the Aleph, in the Hebrew language? What was the Aleph? It was wonder as manifested in the human being.

Now I should like to remind you of something which could lead you to an understanding of all that is really indicated by the sound *a*, all that the sound *a* really signifies. In ancient Greece there was a saying: philosophy begins with wonder. Philosophy, the love of wisdom, the love of knowledge, begins with wonder. Had one spoken absolutely organically, really in accordance with ancient understanding, with ancient instinctive, clairvoyant understanding, one might equally well have said: philosophy begins with *a*. To ancient humanity this would have meant exactly the same thing. Philosophy, love of wisdom, begins with *a*.

But what is it that one is really investigating when one studies philosophy? When all is said and done one is really investigating the human being. Philosophy strives after self-knowledge, and this self-observation begins with the sound *a*. It is, however, at the same time a most profound mystery, for it requires great effort, great activity, to attain to such knowledge of the human being. When the human being approaches his own being and sees how it is formed out of body, soul and spirit, when he looks upon his own being in its entirety, then he is confronted by something before which he will say *a* with the deepest wonder. For this reason *a* corresponds to the human being in a state of wonder, to the human being filled with wonder at his own true being, that is to say, the human being looked at from the highest, most ideal aspect.

The realization that the human being, as he stands before us as a physical being, is only a part of the complete human being, and that we only have the real human being before us when we perceive the full measure of the divine within him, this realization, this wonder called up in us by a contemplation of our own being, was called by ancient humanity: *a*. A corresponds to the human being in his highest perfection. Thus *a* is the human being, and in the sound *a* we are expressing something which is felt in the depths of the human soul. Let us pass over from *a* to *b*, in order to give at least some indication of that which might lead to an understanding of this primal Word which is made up of the entire alphabet. In *b* we have a so-called consonant; in *a* we are dealing with a vowel sound. You will feel if you pronounce a vowel sound that you are giving expression to something coming from the inmost depths of your own being. Every vowel, as we have already seen in the case of the vowel *a*, is bound up with an experience of the soul. In every case where the sound *a* makes its appearance, we have the feeling of wonder. In every case where an *e* makes its appearance we have an experience that can be expressed somewhat as follows: becoming aware that something has been done to me.

Just think for a moment what creatures of abstraction we have become, how withered and lifeless our nature.

Just as an apple or a plum may shrivel up, so have we become shrivelled up as regards our experience of language. When we speak, let us consider how, when we pronounce the sound *a* and proceed from this sound to the sound *e* (which constantly happens), we have no idea that we are passing over from the feeling of wonder to the feeling: I become aware that something has been done to me. Let us now enter into the feeling of the *i* sound. With *i* we have the feeling that we have been curious about something and that our curiosity has been satisfied. A wonderful and far from simple experience lies at the back of every vowel sound. When we allow the five vowel sounds to work upon us we receive the impression of the human being in his primal strength and vigour. We might say that the human being is born again in his true dignity when he allows these five sounds consciously to work upon him, that is to say, when he allows these sounds to proceed out of his inmost being in full consciousness. Therefore it is true to say that we have become quite shrivelled up and think only of the meaning of a word, utterly disregarding the experience behind it. We think only of the meaning. The word 'water' for instance means some particular thing and so on. We have become utterly shrivelled up.

The consonants are quite different in their nature to the vowels. With the consonants we do not feel that the sounds arise from our inmost experience, but we feel that they are images of that which is outside our own being.

Let us suppose that I am filled with wonder, that I say *a*.

I cannot make an outer image of the sound *a*, I must give utterance to it. If, however, I wanted to give expression to something which is round in its form, like this table, for example, what must I do if I do not wish to express it in words? I must imitate it, I must copy its form [corresponding gesture]. If I wanted to describe a nose without speaking, without actually saying the word 'nose' but still wishing to make myself understood, I can copy its form [corresponding gesture]. And it is just the same when the consonants are formed. In the consonants we have an imitation of that which exists in the external world. They are always an imitation of external forms. But we express these forms by constructing them in the air, producing them by means of the larynx and its neighbouring organs, the palate, for example. With the help of these organs we create a form that imitates, copies something that exists outside ourselves. This is carried as far as into the actual form of the letters, but of this we shall speak later.

When we form a *b* (it is, by the way, impossible to pronounce this sound without the addition of some vowel), it is the imitation of something in the external world. If we were able to hold fast the form in the air which is created by *b* (we must, of course, speak the sound aloud) we should have something in the nature of a shelter. A protecting, sheltering form would be produced. Something would be produced that might be likened to a hut or a house. *B* is an imitation of a house. Thus when we begin with *a*, *b*, we have, as it were, the human being in his perfection, and the human being in his house: *a*, *b*.

And so, if we were to go through the whole alphabet, we would unfold the mystery of the human being in the consecutive sounds. We would express the human being as he lives in the cosmos, the human being in his house, his physical body. If we were to pass from *a*, *b*, to *c*, *d*, and so on, every sound would tell us something about the human being. And on reaching *z* we would have pictured in sound the whole of human wisdom, for this is contained in the etheric body of the human being.

We see from this that something of the very greatest significance takes place in speech. In speech the human being himself is fashioned. And one can indeed give a fairly complete picture of the soul life of the human being when one brings to expression his most fundamental feelings. *I, O, A.* These sounds represent practically the whole content of the human soul in its feeling aspect: *I, O, A.*

Let us for a moment consider all that proceeds from the human being when he speaks. Let us suppose that somebody repeats the alphabet; when this is done the entire etheric body of the person comes into being, proceeding from the larynx as from the womb. The etheric body is brought into being. When we look at the physical body of the human being, we know that it has come from the mother, it has come from a metamorphosis of the larynx, that is to say, from the mother's womb.

But now let us picture to ourselves the complete human being as he comes into the world with all his different attributes; for that which is produced by the organism of the mother cannot remain unchanged. If the human being were to remain unchanged throughout his life, he could not be said to be a human being in the true sense of the word; one thing must be continually added to another. The human being at the age of 35, let us say, has gained more from the universal, cosmic being than he had as a child. We may picture the whole human being in some such way as this. Just as speech proceeds from the larynx, the child from the womb, so the fully developed human being at about the age of 35 is born out of the cosmos in the same way in which the words that we speak are spoken out of us. Thus we have the form of the human being, the complete human form, as a spoken word.

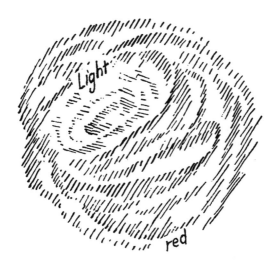

The human form—that most wonderful of earthly forms—stands before us and we ask the divine spiritual powers, which have existed from the beginning: how did you create the human being in a similar way as the spoken word is created when we speak? How did you create the human being? What really took place when you created the human being? And if we were to receive an answer to our question from out of space, it would be some such answer as this. All around us there is movement, form, constantly changing and of infinite variety: such a form [*a* was here shown in eurythmy], such a form [*e* was shown], such a form [*i* was shown]—all variations of form in motion proceed from out of the universe, every possibility of movement that we out of the nature of our being are able to conceive and to bring into connection with the human organization.

My dear friends, we can indeed say that these possibilities of movement are those which, becoming fixed, give the human being his physical form as it is when he reaches full maturity. What, then, would the gods do if they really wished to create the human being out of a lump of earth? The gods would make movements, and as a result of these movements, capable of giving form to the dust of the earth, the human form would eventually arise.

Now let us picture once more the eurythmy movements for *a, b, c,* and so on. Let us imagine that the gods, out of their divine primal activity were to make those eurythmy movements which correspond to the sounds of the alphabet. Then, if these movements were impressed into physical matter, the human being would stand before us. This is what really lies behind eurythmy. The human being as we see him is a completed form. But the form has been created out of movement. It has arisen from those primal forms which were continually taking shape and passing away again. Movement does not proceed from quiescence; on the contrary, that which is in a state of rest originates in movement. In eurythmy we are really going back to primal movement.

What is it that my Creator, working out of primal, cosmic being, does in me as the human being?

To answer this question, you would have to make the eurythmy movements. God makes eurythmy, and as the result of his eurythmy there arises the form of the human being.

What I have said here about eurythmy can indeed be said about any of the arts, for in some way or another every art springs from a divine origin. But because it makes use of the human being as its instrument, one is able to penetrate most deeply through eurythmy into the connection existing between the human being and the cosmic being. For this reason one cannot fail to appreciate eurythmy. For just suppose that one had no real conception of the nature of human beauty, as this is expressed in the outward human form, and then suppose that one had the opportunity of being shown how in the beginning God created the beautiful human form out of movement, and one saw the repetition of those divine creative movements in the eurythmy gestures, then one would receive the answer to the question: how did human beauty come into being?

Let us think of the child, the incomplete human being, who has not yet attained his full adulthood. How can we help the gods, so that the physical form of the child will be properly furthered in its development? What can we bring to the child in the way of movement? We must teach him eurythmy, for this is a continuation of divine movement, of the divine creation of the human being.

And when an illness overtakes the human being, the forms corresponding to his divine archetype have been injured; here, in the physical world, they have changed. What shall we do then? We must go back to those divine movements; we must help the sick human being to make those movements for himself. This will work on him in such a way that the harm his bodily form may have received will be remedied.

Thus we have to look upon eurythmy as an art of healing, just as in ancient clairvoyant times it was known that certain sounds, uttered with a special intonation, had an effect on human health. But in those days one was shown how to affect health by a roundabout way, by means of the air which worked back again into the etheric body. If one works more directly, if one makes the patient actually do the movements corresponding to the formation of his organs, then there arises this third aspect of eurythmy, eurythmy therapy. The point here, of course, is that a person knows what these movements really are, for example certain move-

ments of the foot and leg correspond to certain formations right up in the head.

This introduction was necessary in order that all of you,
as active eurythmists, should gain a fundamental feeling
and perception of what you are doing. You must not take
eurythmy as something that can be learned in the ordinary
conventional way, but you must think of it as something
that brings the human being nearer to the divine than
would otherwise be possible. The same applies indeed to
all art. You must permeate yourselves through and
through with this feeling. What, then, should be considered as an essential part of all eurythmy teaching? The
right atmosphere must enter into it, the feeling for the
connection between the human being and the divine
spiritual powers. This is essential if you would become
eurythmists in the true sense.

2. School eurythmy — a kind of spiritual gymnastics

Rudolf Steiner collaborated with teachers in 1919 to found the first Waldorf school in Stuttgart, Germany. Already at that beginning, eurythmy was included in the curriculum for all the grades. This was a new direction for the eurythmy work. Until then, eurythmy had developed as a performing art. School eurythmy helps children express in movement what the soul is experiencing, for example in geometry lessons, astronomy or history. There is another system of movement known as Eurhythmics, created by Swiss composer Emile Jaques-Dalcroze around 1903 to help musicians and music students develop a better sense of rhythm. That, however, has nothing to do with Steiner.

The lectures in this section speak extensively about the eurythmy figures. These are Steiner's unique creations: two-dimensional wooden 'moving sculptures' that serve as study guides for vowels and consonants, soul moods, and the major and minor common chords. Eurythmy teachers, students in training and students in the upper grades of a Waldorf school use them to discover and refine the inner nature of a gesture.

The figures, 35 in all, are painted in three or four colours, each colour indicating a specific quality of movement. In the typical figure, one of the colours, called the character, represents an intensification of tension in the moving muscle. The excerpt on colour from the Light Course helps us understand how a colour process can be active in the muscle.

The lecture 'Supersensory physiology' was given to teachers of the Stuttgart Waldorf school, September 1920. It includes an important teachers' meditation in three parts: seeing or hearing, comprehending, and remembering.

Education towards inner freedom

The Waldorf school is an organism complete and whole in itself, and if it is not thought of as such, many of its educational principles may be misunderstood. People may think, for instance, that if they go to the school two or three times and see what is done on these particular days that is sufficient; they have seen how we teach at the Waldorf school. That, of course, is not the case. They have seen nothing of any consequence. What they have seen is like a fragment cut out of a picture from which they then proceed to form an opinion of the whole. Suppose you take a fragment of some great picture and show it to someone. How can he form any opinion of the whole picture from this one fragment? The essential feature of Waldorf school education is that every activity has its place within the organism of the whole school. People will understand the Waldorf school much better by studying its principles, its whole structure—the organic connection between the eighth class and the fourth class, for instance, or between the first and the tenth—than by acquainting themselves with one isolated fragment of the teaching. The organization of the school is conceived in such a way that each activity has its rightful place and time and fits in with the whole. And it is from this point of view that individual subjects of instruction are introduced into the school. Let me give an example by briefly describing in principle how eurythmy is given its place in the work as a whole. It is no good setting out to discover things which may then be introduced into the school activities. It is, as a rule, a wrong principle to think out certain things that are good for children — as has happened too frequently in the Froebel kindergarten[1] system — and then set them up as an essential part of education. Nothing should be artificially introduced into the school; it should all proceed from life itself. The teacher should have a free, unprejudiced outlook on life, an understanding of life, and be able to teach and educate children to prepare them for life. The more intimately the teacher is connected with the surrounding life, the better for the school. Narrow-minded teachers who know nothing of life except the school itself can do little to develop the full adulthood of a human being. Eurythmy was introduced into the Waldorf school not because we thought gymnastic exercises were necessary for the children and so set about inventing something. No, indeed! Eurythmy did not arise, to begin with, as an educational measure at all. It arose as the result of certain connections of destiny, about the year 1912, but primarily as an art, not as an educational measure at all. And there will always be an imperfect idea of eurythmy as applied in education if it is thought of as a special educational eurythmy, distinct from eurythmy as an art. For this reason, I myself should have thought it much better if the demonstrations of eurythmy as an art had been given here first, for that would have shown the underlying concept. Because eurythmy is an art, it is part of life and this part of life has been put into a form suitable for educational purposes. Nobody can understand eurythmy as performed by children who fails to realize that it will become art — and perhaps more than many people think, already is today.

Eurythmy as an art came into being about the year 1912, but to begin with only as an art. The Waldorf school began in 1919, and because we found that the art of eurythmy can be applied in the education of children we introduced it into the school. That, however, is secondary. Such circumstances should be understood as applying in everything else if we want to understand the Waldorf school in its relation to life. It is not a question of creating a special method of teaching children to paint, for instance; if we want them to learn how to paint, the principles of the teaching should be drawn from the living art of painting and not from methods that have been specially put together for the purpose of education.

The element of real art must be introduced into schools, not an intellectual substitute for art. And with eurythmy it is indeed possible to infuse art into human culture once again.

In the addresses given before the performances, I

explained the sense in which eurythmy is visible speech—
speech expressed in movement. I only want now to add
something about these figures, for this will additionally
explain the relationship of eurythmy to art. The idea of the
figures came, in the first place, from Miss Maryon[2] but
they have been carried out in the form which I think right
and in strict accordance with the laws of eurythmy.

Here [showing a figure], you have a picture of the
sound S. The figure does in a sense represent a human
being, but those who imagine a beautiful human form in
the sense of modern civilization and convention will not
find much beauty in the figure. They will see nothing of
what strikes them as beautiful in a person they meet in the
street, perhaps. Now when it comes to making such
figures, we may also have an eye for the beauty of the
human form, but the object in this case is to represent what
comes to expression in eurythmy, namely, the human
being in movement. And so in these figures we have
ignored everything that does not belong to the nature and
form of the movement itself, the feeling corresponding to
the particular movement, penetrating the basic character
expressed by and colouring the movement. When you
sing, you take into your whole organism—in a bodily
sense—the elements that move the soul. The movement
takes its course entirely within the limits of the skin and
remains invisible, flowing wholly into the tone that is
heard.

The figure you see here[3] expresses music in movement.
What the soul feels releases itself from the human being,

becomes movement in space and the artistic element expresses itself in the form of the movement. We see what we otherwise hear. And so these figures are only intended to draw attention to what the human being becomes in doing eurythmy, quite separate from the attributes which nature imparts to him. Each movement is then indicated by the shape of the figure and the wood is painted with a certain basic colour. We have written at the back of the figures the names of the colours corresponding to the movements themselves and to the feeling inherent in these movements. The way in which the eurythmists on the stage manipulate their veils is really a continuation of the movement. When the eurythmists have learnt to do this skilfully, the veil will float freely, be drawn back, caught up or given a definite form at the right moment. The movement carried out by the limbs underlies the feeling, which is then expressed by the manipulation of the veil; the feeling comes to expression in the floating veil. If the eurythmist has true feeling for the movement of arms or legs, the quality will instinctively pass over into the manipulation of the veil, the feeling that should accompany the movement in the handling of the veil will be felt.

Thirdly, when this movement [pointing to the figure] is being made, the eurythmist must be able to feel that the arm is stretching out lightly in this direction, as though it were hovering in the air without inner tension. In the other arm, she must feel as if she is summoning all her muscular force and packing it all tightly into the arm. One arm (the right) is held lightly upwards; the left arm is tense, and the muscles are almost throbbing. That is how the movement is given character, and this character in the movement makes an impression on the spectators. They feel what the eurythmist is doing.

Now when the people look at these figures, they may ask where is the face shown and where the back of the head. That, however, has nothing to do with eurythmy. You will sometimes find people who are enthusiastic over the pretty face of a eurythmist, but that, I assure you, is no part of eurythmy! The face on this figure here, which seems as you look at it to be turned to the left, is really facing you, and the colour is used to emphasize that the eurythmist should feel the forces of eurythmy lightly diffused over the right side of the head while the left side of the head is tense, penetrated by inner strength. It is as though the head becomes asymmetrical—relaxed, as if slackened on the one side, taut on the other.

In this way the movements receive their true character. These figures here express what ought to become visible in eurythmy. The same principles hold good in all artistic work. One ought to be able to look away from the substance, the content, the prose, and enter into the artistic, poetic element. The beautiful face of a eurythmist really corresponds to the prose quality. What she expresses when the right side of her head is lightly diffused with eurythmy forces and the left side is tense—that is what constitutes the real beauty in eurythmy. So we can conceive that quite a plain face may be eurythmically beautiful and a beautiful face ugly!

In eurythmy, then, we have elements that hold good for all art — as every artist will agree. A great artist is not merely one who can paint a beautiful girl's face pleasingly. A true artist must, under certain conditions, also be able to paint an old, wizened, wrinkled face in such a way that it becomes artistically beautiful. This must underlie all art.

I wanted to add these remarks about the eurythmy you have seen in the performances here. Let me only say now that we have introduced eurythmy into our Waldorf school because it affords such a wonderful contrast to ordinary gymnastics. As already indicated, bodily exercises are adequately carried out in the Waldorf school, but as regards ordinary, external gymnastics, we elaborate them in such a way that with every exercise the child is first given a sense of space, of the directions of space, which are there of course as the primary thing. The child feels the direction of space and then his arms follow it. In his gymnastics he gives himself over to space. This is the only healthy basis for gymnastic exercises. Space is conditioned in all directions. To our abstract conception of space, there are three directions which we can in no way distinguish. They are only there in geometry. In reality, however, the head is above, the legs below — there we have the above and below. Then we have right and left. We live in this direction of space when we stretch out our arms. The point is not to ask: where is the absolute direction? Of course we can turn this way or that. And then we have our forwards and backwards direction, front and behind. All other directions of space are oriented with respect to these. If we understand space in this way, we can discover really healthy movements for gymnastics, where the human being gives himself up, as it were, to the laws of space.

In eurythmy, the character of the movement is determined by the human organism. And then the question is: what is the soul experiencing in any given movement? This indeed underlies the eurythmy movements for the different sounds. What is happening when the forces of your being flow into the limbs? In ordinary gymnastic exercises the human being lends himself to space; in eurythmy he carries out movements that express his being and are in accordance with the laws of his organism. To allow what is inward to express itself outwardly in movement — that is the essence of eurythmy. To fill the outer with the human being so that the human being unites himself with the outer world — that is the essence of gymnastics.

To educate the whole human being, we can therefore derive gymnastics from the opposite pole to that of eurythmy, where the movements emerge entirely from the inner being of the person; but in any case, even where it is applied in education, the eurythmy element itself must be derived from a true grasp of the artistic principles of eurythmy.

My opinion is that the best teachers of gymnastics are those who have learnt from art. The impulses underlying the gymnastics of Greek schools[4] and the Olympic Games were derived from art. And if the consequences of what I have said are fully realized and all school work is based primarily upon the element of art, we shall apply what I have explained by the example of eurythmy to other branches of life and activity as well. We shall not set out to invent something specifically for teaching, but rather to imbue the school with real life. And then from out of the school life within the social order will grow.

Bothmer gymnastics and eurythmy

Thursday, 1 March 1923, 6.30 p.m.–8 p.m.
At the beginning, Count Fritz von Bothmer[5] gave a lecture about teaching gymnastics with approximately the following content:

Exercises: *Conscious penetration of the body with the child's forces of life. The close connection to eurythmy. Eurythmy enlivens, gymnastics carries those forces into the outermost limbs through the will. Eurythmy is not done as consciously. There are movements that can give the impression of death or make things alive. The relationship of gymnastics to experiencing growth and to opening of the body. The gymnastics teacher works like a sculptor with the child. Guidelines about how to act in the class. Children doing gymnastics feel their way into the room. Children should have a strong inner contact with the dimensions of the room. Squatting on the earth or jumping away from it. Experiencing inhaling and exhaling. 'I tell the children to straighten up your head, straighten your back, straighten your shoulders because children have a tendency to let them hang. But*

I am not certain if I should say such things.' In gymnastics, we are particularly concerned with will.

Exercises using equipment: *Modern equipment is mostly dead. Usually it is quite abstract, for example the parallel bars. Fortunately, we do not have a climbing pole. They are completely dead in comparison with the rope. Today, gymnastics on equipment is quite simply routine. With such dead things, the children are not there with their whole being. In order to encompass their whole body, you can combine two devices, for example the horizontal bar and the horse. If you combine two movements at the same time or one directly after the other, gymnastics is much more lively, particularly outdoors. The most beautiful thing is jumping over a ditch and over a hedge. Our children do not have much opportunity to exercise in that way.*

Games and sports: *Dr Steiner has said that too many games make children too soft. We don't have time for that. Sports such as swimming, shot-put, throwing the discus or javelin should be emphasized over other, more external sports. Emphasize the beauty of the movement and not simply breaking a record.*

Should boys and girls participate together or exercise in the same room, but separately? Girls hold the boys up. Should we group the children according to their temperaments? That would be the ideal.

Dr Steiner: Perhaps I can say something more general about gymnastics later. When we have time before the beginning of the new school year, I can discuss gymnastic exercises in relationship to the child's age and how to make them complete. That is what we will do. Today, I would like to speak about what you just presented. If I do not mention something, please consider that to mean that I agree with you on that point. I will not focus on anything I agree with.

Concerning the relationship of gymnastics to eurythmy, there cannot actually be any conflict between gymnastics and eurythmy. In general, we can see gymnastics exercises and how they are presented as a continuation of eurythmy exercises. Suppose we take a particular movement of the arm in eurythmy and a corresponding movement in gymnastics. In eurythmy we need to take care that the form of the movement itself lies nearer the centre of the body than it would in gymnastics. Thus, there can actually be no conflict.

You can best understand that when you realize that in eurythmy you are primarily concerned with that part of the human organism which is directly connected with the inner breathing process. Thus what an arm or leg, a finger or toe does in eurythmy is directly connected with what occurs as the inner breathing process, the process of the transition from air to blood. On the other hand, what happens in gymnastics is primarily connected with the human organic process based on the transition from blood to muscle. That is primarily physiological and sheds complete light on the development of the muscles. As soon as we understand that instinctively or intuitively, we will see that every movement in gymnastics is connected with strengthening the muscles, with their growth, and with making them elastic by forcing blood into them. The more you understand that, the more you will be able to develop free exercises.

We can make the same point from a different perspective. Eurythmy is primarily a pliable forming of the organism. Or I could also say that eurythmy exists in the sculpting of the organism. Gymnastics lives in the static forces and the dynamics of the organism. Of course, you, Count Bothmer, experienced this when you mentioned that the children feel the room during gymnastics. You can best understand this through the picture of how an arm or leg moves in space, or their relationships to weight.

We can see that there is no conflict with eurythmy if we take character into account. We do that much too little in educational eurythmy because it is not so important in artistic presentations, but it is much more important in education. If you have seen the eurythmy figures, you will have noticed that we differentiate between movement, feeling and character. In movement and feeling, which you have taken into account almost exclusively, things are going well. However, character has not permeated eurythmy movements to any great extent. That is natural because it has no great importance in artistic eurythmy, which is viewed by others.

In contrast, the character of a movement should play a significant part in educational eurythmy. A person doing eurythmy should feel how a movement or position flows back into their own feeling. For example, such a person should feel the pressure of one limb upon another in a eurythmy movement and how that pressure flows back into the centre of the body. For that reason, I coloured the eurythmy figures so that it would be clear. You will find three colours in all the eurythmy figures. One is for the movement, the second, which is like a veil over the first, is for feeling, and the third is for character. For a person doing eurythmy, it indicates the specific part of the body where the muscles should be tensed, and the feeling which such muscle tension should produce. That is part of how eurythmy lives in the shape of the body.

The students have asked if we could present the figures during the education week at Easter, so I will bring them here. We should have such a series here. The Waldorf teachers should study those figures because they are also important for a more psychological physiology. The Waldorf teachers should study them to gain greater understanding of the human organism. At the same time, they can form the basis of a more general feeling for art, for a greater understanding of the inner aspects of the human organism.

We can, therefore, say that the gymnastics teacher should have an idea of the spiritual relationship of the static and dynamic forces in the human organism. The gymnastics teacher should have a clear picture of what it means to raise a leg or to drop an arm in relationship to gravity. On the other hand, the eurythmy teacher should have a strong feeling for what will develop the limbs sculpturally. It is incorrect to say that the gymnastics teacher is like a sculptor. That would be true for the eurythmy teacher. The work of gymnastics teachers is to picture an ideal human being in terms of lines, forms and movements into which they must develop these lazy, sloppy people they have before them. You were certainly correct when you mentioned how children should carry themselves. Whereas the eurythmy teacher should work so that the muscles feel themselves, feel how they gain strength through the character of the movement, the gymnastics teacher should feel how people can properly perceive the heaviness or lightness of a limb. The child should learn, not through reason, but instinctively, how to perceive the lifting of an arm or leg in relationship to gravity. Children should, for example, develop a feeling for how their foot becomes heavy when they stand on one leg and lift the other. The task of the gymnastics teacher is, therefore, to place the dynamic ideal human being he or she carries in his or her soul into another person. Of course, the artistic element must also play a role, since we can realize human static or dynamic forces only through artistic feeling. Whereas, artistic feeling plays a major role in the sculpting activity of eurythmy, it must precede the forms the gymnastics teacher creates in terms of static and dynamic forces.

Concerning the question of breathing, it is significant that eurythmy lies closer to the breath, whereas gymnastics lies closer to the blood process. Aside from the fact that the tempo of breathing increases during the course of the exercises, something that is a physiological process, it is important that we should develop gymnastic technique in such a way that it does not affect the breathing process.

We could call a gymnastics exercise incorrect if, while maintaining the proper physical position, the exercise negatively affects the breathing process. We should exclude those gymnastic exercises that disturb the breathing process, even though the body is properly held. Now that I have seen everything you are doing, it seems to me that all the breathing exercises in modern gymnastic methods are directed towards maintaining proper posture, and that breathing is treated as a reaction. I have noticed that all the things presented are directed primarily towards creating proper posture, at least to the extent that it is expressed through the breathing process. That is something Swedish gymnastics for the most part takes into account. That is what I want to say about that.

In gymnastics, it is important that we take the will into account. The teacher must, therefore, whether instinctively or intuitively, directly access the connection between movements of the body and expressions of the will. The teacher must have a feeling for what the connection between movement and will is. In eurythmy, there is also a development of will, but one that uses a more indirect path through inner feeling and occurs at a level where will is expressed through feeling. That is what I just referred to as character, and it is the experience of feeling in an act of will.

The gymnastics teacher works directly with the act of will, but the eurythmy teacher works with experiencing the feeling in an act of will. You can see how there is everywhere a very strict separation and we need to take that into account when developing a curriculum. Perhaps we cannot immediately do that, but we should certainly see it as our ideal. Then, from these two things we will clearly see why it is much easier for girls in eurythmy and for boys in gymnastics. Things are more clearly differentiated with boys. For that reason we will, in fact, have to allow the boys and girls to do their gymnastics in the same room, but in different groups. The girls can form a group for themselves and do those exercises that create a relationship between them. If we do such exercises that are modified for boys and girls, they will enjoy them more.

I think this will become apparent when we discuss the curriculum in detail. The same is also true of the differences in age.

Concerning exercises with equipment, I would like to remark that we could modify the form of the equipment and make it more appropriate. In that way, at least to a certain extent, we can make the most common pieces of equipment not quite so bad, so we can do something with them. Although I do not want to be fanatical about this, I would also like to see that we have no climbing poles, but I don't want to complain about them too much.

Anyone who has observed what boys in the villages do when a tree is brought from the woods and placed on top of a pole on a church holiday will know how valuable such climbing poles can be. Up at the top, a few branches remain with a small kerchief, a sweet, or maybe a small bottle of wine attached, and the boys have to climb their way up to that little tree attached to the top of the pole from which the bark has been removed. The victor is the boy who brings it down. That very strongly connects the activity of the will to the nature of the body. We do this same thing artificially with a climbing pole. It is certainly better when the children have to learn how to climb a rope. The pole has a rather limited significance in gymnastics, I would say, but I do not want to completely remove it. With the parallel and high bars, with the horse and so on, you can certainly gain something from them if they are properly used.

I also agree you should do the exercises, at least to an extent, by combining the different pieces of equipment, because that emphasizes what equipment exercises should achieve, namely, more presence of mind. That has a secondary effect of also strengthening the muscles. The children thus develop proper strength and elasticity.

I also agree that the high bar should be more prominent, and that it will gain that through a kind of scrutiny, not scrutiny with the eyes, but through the body. One useful exercise would be to have the children swing so they must then catch the bar. They would need to hold themselves in the air. That is only an example to indicate the direction of my thinking. It could be done with the hands or also with the entire arms, but the movement really becomes significant only if it is done with the arms. You could, however, allow the children to begin with their hands.

These things that allow the children to feel the device with their entire body can also give them a greater sympathy for the equipment. That is particularly true with the high bar when the children learn to work on it with their legs. You could combine exercises with the high bar by first having them do what I mentioned above and then having them 'walk' the bar with their legs dangling. All of this simply gives some idea of the direction. I don't think I need to speak about dead equipment and simple routine. That is the way things were, but things do not need to be routine when we emphasize this way of experiencing the equipment. The children can use their legs in wonderful ways on the bars.

I completely agree with what you said about games and sports. Our gymnastics should lead to what you described.

We will discuss the gymnastics curriculum at the next opportunity. Then, we will also consider the temperaments at various ages.

Discussions with teachers

T. spoke about the children who are not good at Arithmetic.

Rudolf Steiner: If you discover a special weakness in arithmetic, it will be good to proceed as follows. As a rule, the other children will have two gymnastics lessons in the week, or rather one eurythmy lesson and one gymnastics lesson. You can assemble a group of the children who are not good at arithmetic and let them have an extra hour or half-hour of eurythmy or gymnastics. This need not mean a lot of extra work for you; you can take them with others who are doing the same kind of exercises, but you must try to improve these children's capacities by means of gymnastics and eurythmy. First give them rod exercises. Tell them: 'Hold the rod in your hand, first in front counting 1, 2, 3; then behind 1, 2, 3, 4.' Each time the child must change the position of the rod, moving it from front to back. He must make a great effort in some way to get the rod behind him at 3. Then add walking, say, 3 steps forwards, 5 steps backwards; 3 steps forwards, 4 steps backwards; 5 steps forwards, 3 steps backwards and so on. Try in gymnastics, and also perhaps in eurythmy, to combine number with the child's movements, so that he is obliged to count while he is moving. You will find that this has an effect. I have frequently done this with pupils.

But now tell me: why does it have an effect? From what you have already learnt you should have some ideas about it.

A teacher said: eurythmy movements must be a great help in the teaching of geometry.

Rudolf Steiner: But I did not mean geometry. What I said applies to arithmetic because what lies at the root of arithmetic is consciously willed movement, the sense of movement. When you activate the sense of movement in this way you will enhance a child's arithmetical powers.

First grade Waldorf students.
'... an infinite amount of good can be achieved by permeating the bodies of little children with elementary eurythmy ... They could overcome a kind of heaviness that lives in the limbs.'
Practical Advice to Teachers

You bring something up out of the subconscious which in such a child does not want to be brought up. Speaking generally, if a child is bad both at arithmetic and geometry this should be remedied by exercises in movement. You will be able to do a great deal for a child's progress in geometry with varied and inventive eurythmy exercises, and rod exercises also.

Boys and girls at the Waldorf school

Let me now say a few words on the significance of
eurythmy teaching and the educational value of eurythmy
for the child. In illustration of what I have to say, I should
like to use these figures made in the Dornach studio.[6]
They are artistic representations of the real content of
eurythmy. The immediate object of these figures is to help
in the appreciation of artistic eurythmy. But I shall be able
to make use of them to explain some things in educational
eurythmy. Now, eurythmy is essentially a visible speech,
it is not miming, not pantomime,* neither is it an art of

---

*Rudolf Steiner uses different words for mime and pantomime in the
German texts. The reader may assume he is distinguishing the two from
each other, and both from what he intended as eurythmy. Pantomime, or
fabula saltica, was the creation of the ancient Roman theatre around the
time of the Late Republic. There were three kinds of drama – tragedy, the
satyr play and comedy. The new pantomimes, comic at first, were performed less often as such the more pantomime grew to gradually relegate
traditional tragedy to the background. A solo pantomime actor performed a number of roles in succession while the drama's text was sung
by a whole chorus. The actor's many roles were portrayed only by artistic
movements. The chorus for pantomime solos stood unseen, behind side
screens, allowing the full attention of the audience to focus on the soloist.
The pantomime actors wore masks on their heads. Pantomime is easily
confused with mime, an older dramatic form. Mime in the ancient theatre
was a maskless farce, more a comedy, and was acted with dancing or
acrobatics. For more on mime and pantomime, the reader may refer to
The Ancient Theatre by Erika Simon, Methuen & Co. Ltd., London/New
York 1982, p. 36.

dance. When a person sings or speaks he produces activity and movement in certain organs; this same movement which is inherent in the larynx and other speech organs is capable of being continued and manifested throughout the human being. In the speech organs the movements are arrested and repressed. For instance, an activity of the larynx which would issue in this movement (*A*) — where the wings of the larynx open outward — is submerged in *status nascendi* and transformed into a movement into which the meaning of speech can be put — and into a movement that can pass out into the air and be heard. Here you have the original movement of *A* (ah), the inner and essentially human movement, as we might call it.

This is the movement that comes from the whole human being when he expresses *A* (ah). Thus there is a movement which is arrested in *status nascendi*[7] for every utterance in speech and song. But it seeks to come to expression in forms of movement made by the whole human being. These are the forms of utterance in movements, and they can be discovered.

Just as there are different forms of the larynx and other organs for *A* (ah), *I* (ee), *L*, *M*, there are also corresponding movements and forms of movement. These forms of movement are therefore those expressions of will which otherwise are provided in the expressions of thought and will of speech and song. The thought element, the abstract part of the thinking in speech, is here removed and all that is to be expressed is transposed into the movement. Hence eurythmy is an art of movement, in every sense of the word. Just as you can hear the *A*, so can you see it; just as you can hear the *I*, so can you see it.

In these figures the form of the wood is intended to express the movement. The figures are made on a three-colour principle. The fundamental colour here is the one that expresses the form of the movement. But just as feeling pervades the tones of speech, so feeling enters into the movement. We do not merely speak a sound, we colour it by feeling. We can also do this in eurythmy. In this way a strong unconscious momentum plays into eurythmy. If the performer, the eurythmist, can bring this feeling into his movements in an artistic way the onlookers will be affected by it as they watch the movements.

It should be borne in mind, moreover, that the veil which is worn serves to enhance the expression of feeling, it accompanies and moves in accordance with the feeling. This was brought out in the performance over there [Tr. note: e.g. at Keble College]. As you see here in the figures, the second colour—which comes mainly on the veils—represents the feeling nuance in the movement. Thus you have a first, fundamental colour expressing the movement itself, and a second colour over it, mainly falling on the veil, which expresses the nuance of feeling. But the eurythmy performer must have the inner power to impart the feeling to his movement, just as it makes a difference whether I say to a person 'come here' as a command, or 'come here' as a friendly request. This is the nuance of feeling, gradation of feeling. What I say is different if I say 'come here' as a command or 'come here' as a friendly request. In the same way this second colour, here expressed as blue on a foundation of green which then continues over into the veil [Tr. note: where it becomes pure blue], represents the feeling nuance in the language of eurythmy.

And the third thing that is brought out is character, a strong element of will. This can only be introduced into eurythmy when the performer is able to experience his own movements as he makes them and express them strongly in himself. The way a performer holds his head as he does eurythmy makes a great difference to his appearance. Whether, for instance, he keeps the muscles on the left of the head taut and those on the right slack is expressed here by means of the third colour [showing figure]: you see here that the muscles on the left of the head are somewhat tense, those on the right relaxed. You will observe how the third colour always indicates the controlled will. Here you see that the left side and over across the month is somewhat contracted; here [in another figure] the forehead is contracted, the muscles of the forehead are contracted. This, you see, sets the tone for the inner character as a whole, radiating out from such a slight contraction. For this slight contraction radiates throughout the organism. Thus the art of eurythmy is really composed of the movement, expressed in the fundamental colour; of the feeling nuance, expressed by the second colour; and of this element of will. Indeed, the element of art as a whole is will, but will is here emphasized in a special way.

Where the object is to exhibit the features of eurythmy, those parts only of the human being are represented which are characteristic of eurythmy. If we had figures here with beautifully painted noses and eyes and beautiful mouths, they might be charming paintings. But for eurythmy that is not the point; what you see painted, modelled or carved here is solely what belongs to the art of eurythmy in the human being doing eurythmy.

A human being performing eurythmy has no need to make a special face. That does not matter. Naturally, it goes without saying, a normal and proper eurythmist would not make a disagreeable face when making a kindly movement, but this would be the same in speaking. No art of facial expression independent of eurythmic expression is required. For instance, a performer can make the *A* movement by turning the axes of his eyes outwards. That is allowable, that is eurythmy. But it would not do if someone were to make a special face as is done in mime; these faces, which are often a special requirement in mime, would here be a grimace. In eurythmy everything must be eurythmic.

Thus we have in these figures a form of art which shows only that part of the human being which is eurythmy, all else is left out; and thus we get an artistic impression. For each art can only express what it has to express through its own particular medium. A statue cannot be made to speak; thus you must bring out the expression of soul you want through the shaping of the mouth and the whole face. It would have been no good in this case, either, to have painted human beings naturalistically; what had to be painted was a direct expression of eurythmy.

Naturally, when I speak of veils this does not mean that one can change the veil with every letter; but one comes to find, by trying out different feeling nuances for a poem and entering into the mood of the poem, that a poem as a whole has an *A* mood or a *B* mood. Then one can perform the whole poem properly in one veil. The same holds good of the colour. Here I have put the veil form, colour, etc. which go together for every letter. There must be a certain fundamental key in a poem. This key is given by the colour of the veil, and in general by the whole colour combination; and this has to be retained throughout the poem, otherwise the ladies would have to be continually changing veils, throwing off veils, putting on other dresses, and things would be even more complicated than they are already and people would say they understood even less. But actually if one once has the fundamental key one can maintain it throughout the whole poem, making the changes from one letter to another, from one syllable to another, from one mood to another by means of the movements.

Now since my aim today is concerned with education, I have here set out these figures in the order in which children learn the sounds. And the first sound the children learn, when they are quite young, is the sound *A*. And they continue in this approximate order, for naturally where children are concerned many digressions occur. But on the whole the children get to know the vowels in this order : *A, E, I, O, U*, the normal order. And then, when the children have to practise the visible speech of eurythmy, when they come to do it in this same order, it is for them like a resurrection of what they felt when they first learned the sounds of speech as little children, a resurrection, a rebirth at another stage. In this language of eurythmy the child experiences what he had experienced earlier. It affirms the power of the word in the child through the medium of the whole being.

Then the children learn the consonants in this order: *M, B, P, D, T, L, N*; there should also be an *NG* here, as in sing, but it has not yet been made. Then *F, H, G, S, R. R*, that mysterious letter which properly has three forms in human speech, is the last one for children to do perfectly. There is a lip *R*, a palatal *R* and a guttural *R*.

Thus what the child learns in speech in the speaking or singing part of his organism can be carried over into the whole being and developed into visible speech.

If there should be a sufficient interest for this expressive art, we could make more figures; joy, sorrow, antipathy, sympathy, for instance, and other things which are all part of eurythmy. And not just grammar, but rhetoric, too, comes into its own in eurythmy. We could make figures for all these things. Then people would see how this soul and spiritual activity, which not only influences the functions of the human being's physical body but develops both his soul and spiritual and organic bodily nature, has a very definite value both in education and as an art.

As to these eurythmy figures, they also serve in the study of eurythmy as a help to the student's memory — for do not

Rudolf Steiner's sketch for a eurythmy figure; handwritten notes indicate colours.

suppose that eurythmy is so easy that it can be learned in a few hours, eurythmy must be thoroughly studied. These figures, then, are useful to students for practising eurythmy and for going more deeply into their art. You can see there is a very great deal in the forms themselves, though they are quite simply made and painted.

I wished today to speak of the art of eurythmy in so far as it forms part of the educational principle of the Waldorf School.

Light Course

Colours arise where dark and light work together. This is what I wanted to make clear to you today. Now if you want to consider for yourselves how you will best understand it, you need only think for instance of how differently your own etheric body interacts with your muscles and your eyes. It interacts with the muscle in such a way as to blend with the functions of the muscle; not so in the eye. The eye being very isolated, the etheric body here does not interact with the physical organ in the same way, but remains comparatively independent. Consequently the astral body can come into very intimate union with the portion of the etheric body that is in the eye. Inside the eye our astral body is more independent, and independent in a different way than in the rest of our physical organization. Let this be the part of the physical organization in a muscle, and this the physical organization of the eye. To describe it we must say: our astral body interacts with both, but in a very different way. In the muscle it interacts in such a way that it goes through the same space as the physical bodily part and is not independent. In the eye too it interacts: here however it works independently. The space is filled by both, in both cases, but in the one case the ingredients work independently while in the other they do not. It is only half the truth to say that our astral body is there in our physical body. We must ask how it is in it, for it is in it differently in the eye and in the muscle. In the eye it is relatively independent, and yet it is in it, no less than in the muscle. You see from this: ingredients can interpenetrate each other and still be independent. So too, you can unite light and dark to get grey; then they are interpenetrating like astral body and muscle. Or on the other hand light and dark can so interpenetrate as to retain their independence, then they are interpenetrating as do the astral body and the physical organization in the eye. In the one instance, grey arises; in the other, colour. When they interpenetrate like the astral body and the muscle, grey arises; whilst when they interpenetrate like the astral body and the eye, colour arises, since they remain relatively independent in spite of being there in the same space.

Wonders of the world

In April of this year there could have been celebrated the half-centenary of an extremely important discovery of modern science, a discovery which, rightly understood, fully confirms the spiritual-scientific doctrine of evolution. Of course spiritual-scientific discoveries can only be made through clairvoyance, but they can be confirmed by the facts that ordinary science brings to light. The fiftieth anniversary of that important dissertation on the speech-centre, which the great doctor and philosopher Broca[8] delivered before the Paris Anthropological Society in April 1861, might well have been celebrated this year. For the work of Broca provides complete proof that the trigger which configures, which forms the specific part of the brain which creates both the aesthetic consciousness of speech and the understanding of its sounds does not reside in the inner laws of the physical brain. When in April 1861 Broca found that the organ of speech lies in the third convolution of the brain, and that this organ must be functioning properly if a person is to understand the sounds of speech, and that another part must also function for him to speak, this discovery constituted an important advance which can be turned to good account by spiritual science. It is a verification of the facts known to it. Why is this? Because the way the speech centre is developed shows that a person's outer movements, the movements of his hands (i.e. what he does half unconsciously) plays a part in the configuration of the speech-centre.

Why is this speech-centre particularly developed on the left side? It is because under the cultural conditions that have prevailed so far, human beings have made particular use of the right hand. Thus it is the etheric and astral bodies, bringing about the movements of the hands out of the unconscious, which work into the brain and mould it. Today the study of the human being makes it plain that the brain is formed from without by macrocosmic forces. When this part of the brain is injured, there is no capacity for speech. If we take into consideration that the side of the brain which through our right-handedness has been strongly developed can be relieved from without by the use of the left hand — something which is still possible in childhood though no longer in later life — then it can be seen that the systematic activity of the brain from without can be so moulded that a speech-centre develops in the corresponding third convolution of the brain on the right side. Must we not say that it is the greatest possible error to think that the faculty of speech is formed through the predisposition of the brain? It is not the natural tendency of the brain which brings into existence the faculty of speech but the activity which the human being himself develops. The faculty of speech is developed in the brain from out of the macrocosm. The organ of speech is the result of speaking, not speaking the result of the speech-organ. That is what has been established through the important physiological facts discovered by Broca. It is because the gods, or the spirits of the hierarchies have helped human beings to carry out the activities which create their speech-centre that the speech-centre has been developed from without. The speech-centre arises from speech, not vice versa.

When rightly understood, all such modern discoveries provide confirmation for spiritual science, and it is a pity that I am never able to do more than make a brief reference to such things. Were I able to speak at greater length about characteristic examples of this kind you would see how short-sighted the people are who say that spiritual science contradicts modern science. On the contrary, it is only at variance with the interpretation placed on the facts by modern scholarship, not at all at variance with the actual facts themselves.

Thus it is the activity of the hierarchies,[9] who have worked into us from without, which has made of our macrocosmic development what we are during earth existence. We are indeed a product of the macrocosm. Today we are a product of the movements of our limbs, of our gestures, which carry on a silent speech; these movements imprint themselves on the brain, which has no prior disposition to speech. The archetypal human being has, of himself, no predisposition to anything, but everything has been formed and developed and bestowed upon him by the macrocosmic activity of the spiritual hierarchies.

The genius of language

In many ways there no longer exists such language that expresses a combination of shades of feeling and sound. We can still find this sometimes in dialects, which also have it in themselves to bring the visual to expression. For instance, you will find in dialect—more often than in educated speech—the occasional phrase *unter den Arm greifen*, 'to help someone' or 'lend a hand', literally 'to reach under someone's arm'. This simply means to come to the aid of a person who needs help. Why? Because a young person, in offering a hand to someone elderly who cannot get about so easily any more, reaches under the other person's arm to give support. This active image was then transferred to any helpful act. Exactly as it was with the expression in Lecture 2 'to wipe the night-sleep out of our eyes', so it is with the act of giving help, a single specific procedure is chosen to express visually a more abstract generality. Sometimes the genius of language has not been able to retain the visual element; alternatively, from time to time imagery has been retained in one instance and cast off in another

There still exists today the word *lauschen* ('listen with inner attentiveness') for a certain kind of listening. The Austrian dialect also has a word related to *lauschen*: *losen*. We not only say in Austria when we want to make a person listen, *Hör einmal* ('listen'), but also *Los amol!* ('take note'). *Losen* is a weaker but still active listening. Educated colloquial German has retained *lauschen*. *Losen* is a cognate with the feeling of a somewhat weak activity, even with a certain sneakiness, pointing to a secret kind of listening. In a sense *losen* has taken on the meaning of forbidden listening. For instance when a person puts his ear to the keyhole or listens in when two others are discussing something not meant for his hearing, then the word *losen* ('take note') is used.

Only after becoming sensitive to the feeling element in such sound sequences can we proceed to develop a sense for the basic sounds, the vowels and consonants. In the Austrian dialect there is a word *Ahnl* for grandmother. Do you perhaps know the word *Ahnl*? A more general term is *Ahnfrau* (*der Ahn*, *die Ahne*, male and female grand-parents/progenitors). In *Ahnl* you have *Ahne* combined with an *l*. If you want to understand what is happening there in the realm of speech, you must rise to a heightened feeling of *l* as a consonant. Feel the *l* in the suffix *-lich* ('-ly', as in friendly) which, as I have explained, has its origins in *leik*. It is somehow related to the feeling that something is moving about, that such moving about has to be imitated in the language. An *Ahnl* is a person who is clearly old but who gives the impression of being lively and mobile, you hardly notice the wrinkles in her face! You see the char-acter of *l* as it is used here.

Take the word *schwinden* 'dwindle, fade': to go away, to make a thing go away so that it can't be seen any more. Now consider that I do not really want to make it go away, but I want to cheat a little in seeming to make it go away. I want to effect something that is not a true, honest dis-appearance – but I also feel a moving around, an *l* as in the *Ahnl* – and there we have the word *schwindeln* 'to swindle'. The *l* makes the difference. You can feel exactly the subtly nuanced value of *l* by going from *schwinden* to *schwindeln*. [Parallels in English would be tramp-trample, side-sidle, tread-treadle.]

If you consider these thoughts, eurythmy[10] will become completely natural. You will feel that eurythmy arises from our ancient, original relationship to the sound elements of words which, if the sound elements are removed, are brought to expression by movement. If you can feel such a thing, then you will be able to sense precisely how, for instance, in the vowel *u* (ooh) there is an element of moving close together, snuggling close up. Look at how you do the *u* in eurythmy [arms and hands are brought close and parallel to each other, as in the written letter]. You have the moving together, the closeness of the gesture, so that we can say that it would be impossible to have an *a* (ah) or *e* (ay) as the strong vowel in the word *Mutter* ('mother'), someone you usually come close to. [The *o* of 'mother' is a gesture of affection]. You can't imagine saying *Metter* or *Matter*. *Mater* shows that the language in which it occurs, Latin, was already a weakened one, the original word was *Mutter*.

I have shown you with all these things the path of the genius of language, a path on which a barrier was erected, as I said, between the sound element of a word and its meaning. They were originally closely united in subjective human perception. They have separated. The sound content has descended into the subconscious, the mental picture has ascended into our consciousness. Much has been cast off that could be perceived when human beings originally lived in close connection with the things and activities around them. When we go back to earlier times in language development, we find the altogether remarkable fact that the original forms of language take us completely out into factual reality, that there existed on the primitive levels of language formation a fine sense for actual facts, and that the people who lived at this level lived closely connected with things and with everything that occurs with things. The moment this living connection is broken, the sense for reality becomes hazy and people live in an unreality that expresses itself in abstract language.

There were three genders in the original Indo-European languages, as in Latin. We still have three genders in German. You can feel three different qualities expressed as masculine, feminine and neuter. In French there are only two genders left, in English only one. This shows us that the English language has divested itself with a grand gesture, one could say, of the sense for reality, that it now merely hovers over things but no longer lives in events. In that early stage of human development, when the gender of words was being formed, there still existed a primitive clairvoyance; a living, spiritual quality was perceived within things. *Der Sonne* ('sun'), masculine, and *die Mond* ('moon'), feminine [which were later reversed to *die Sonne* and *der Mond* in modern German, in which sun is feminine and moon is masculine] could never have come about in the older Indo-European languages had the elemental beings living in the sun and moon not been experienced as brothers and sisters. In antiquity the sun was felt to be the brother, the moon the sister. Today it has been turned around in German. The day was perceived as the son and the night as the daughter of the giant Norwi. This undoubtedly originates from primitive clairvoyant vision. The feeling for the earth at that time was very different from the geologists' perception of it today, when they would actually have good reason to use the neuter gender and speak of *das Erde* [the correct form in modern German is *die Erde*, feminine]. People nowadays no longer sense that the earth is in fact Gaia[11] for whom the masculine god is Uranos.[12] In the areas where the Germanic language was originally formed, people still had a perception of this.

The feeling arising out of the close connection with the world outside was the source for determining gender, for deciding characteristic gender. The elephant (*der Elefant*) was considered strong, the mouse (*die Maus*) weak. Since a man was perceived as strong and a woman as weak, the elephant was given the masculine gender, the mouse the feminine. The trees of the forest are usually feminine because of the original perception that they were the dwelling places of female divinities. Of immense importance, because it points to a deep aspect of the genius of language, is the fact that alongside the masculine and feminine genders there exists a neuter gender. We say *der Mann* (masculine, 'the man'), *die Frau* (feminine, 'the woman'), *das Kind* (neuter, 'the child'). The child's gender or sex is not yet articulated, has not yet reached complete definition, is in the process of becoming. When the neuter gender arose, it came up out of a certain mood in the folk-genius, a feeling that anything given a neuter gender would only later become what it was to be. Gold does not yet have the special characteristic it will have in the future. It is still young in the cosmos, it is not yet what it is destined to be. Hence it is not *der Gold* (masculine) or *die Gold* (feminine) but *das Gold* (neuter).

On the other hand we can look at what comes about when the visualizing power that could characterize gender disappears. We say today *die Mitgift* ('dowry'), which shows a clear connection to an earlier word *die Gift*. We also say today *der Abscheu* ('aversion'), which is clear evidence of an earlier word *der Scheu*. Both these deductions are correct. *Der Scheu* and *die Gift* have gone through a subtle change in connotation. *Die Gift* in early times simply meant 'the noncommittal act of giving'. But because of what some people have given and what was, also in Faust's opinion, harmful to others, the word has changed its meaning and has been applied to gifts that are objectionable, losing the connection with the original gender characteristic. The result is *das Gift* ('poison') with neuter gender. When a person once was called *scheu*, he was considered as having strong feelings, as being firm in himself. When the word became weak, it became *die Scheu* ('shyness'), feminine.

That our language has become more abstract, that it has released itself from its interweaving with outer reality, can best be understood from the fact that the ancient Indo-European languages had eight cases: nominative, genitive, dative, accusative, vocative, ablative, locative and instrumental. This means that not only was the position of a thing expressed as it is done today with the first four cases, but people were also able to follow other relationships with their feelings. For instance, to do a thing at a certain time, we can express as *diesen Tag* ('on this day'), accusative, or *dieses Tages* ('of this day'), genitive. No longer do we experience the active helpfulness of the day, of the time of day, or of a special day in particular. No longer do we have the experience that whatever is done on 2 January 1920, for instance, could not be accomplished later; that time is a helpful element, that time is involved in something that helps us. There existed a feeling for all this in earlier ages when the instrumental case, *hiu tagu*, was used. We would have to say something like *durch diesen Tag* ('through this day'), *vermittelst dieses Tages* ('by means of this day'). *Hiu tagu* has become the word *heute* ('today'). The old instrumental case is buried in the word, just as *hiu jaru* has become *heuer* ('this year'). But German has retained only four cases and cast off the others. You will understand from this how continuously language becomes more and more abstract, and how the capacity for abstract thought with its definite lack of a sense for reality has been taking the place of an earlier connection with the real world. This is what language reveals.

Picture writing, writing, eurythmy

What you will see on the stage is the human being in movement, or groups of human beings in movement. Essentially, the movements you will see are not gestures or mime, nor are they something in the nature of dance, but they are in reality visible speech. And they are real speech, not something based on an interpretation of words or suchlike, but something based on a careful study of the nature of audible speech itself.

In audible speech we are also dealing with movement, movement being carried out by the larynx and other speech organs, which does not however appear as such but is restrained, we might say, in the way it arises and is then transformed into the motion of the air we hear as sound.

Through sensory and supersensory vision—a Goethean expression—we can indeed gain an idea through careful study of how the larynx and the other speech organs try to move, what that inner movement which turns into sound is like and how it arises. And we can then create visible speech through the movement of a single organ or a group of organs of the human body so that the whole human being, and particularly the arms, moves in the same way as the speech organs try to move in audible speech but are prevented from doing so, so that their movement turns into sound.

Now we can say that by turning the whole human being into a larynx, or a group of human beings into a large speech organ, we are able to reveal true artistic sources and an artistic language of forms, also with regard to those things which are expressed through music or poetry. It happens in the following way.

Poets have to express themselves through language. Particularly in more advanced civilizations, language becomes increasingly conventional but it also becomes increasingly an expression of an abstract way of thinking. Neither conventional nor abstract thinking can be artistic in any sort of way. Hence we can say, putting it in superficial terms, that creating poetry in advanced languages becomes increasingly difficult if no other means of expression are used as a help.

It is easier to understand what I mean by visible speech if we think of the other boundary, the inartistic boundary of speech, the opposite boundary to eurythmy (which we will come to shortly).

In a certain sense we can consider writing, fixed on paper, also as a metamorphosis of speech. It is also a kind of visible speech. But writing develops in the opposite direction. We can trace writing back to its original stages. There we can see how the thought, the idea that people formed of a physical object is still present in the written symbol or symbols, how the conceptual element becomes a type of silent speech, a visible speech.

But then the writing which first developed as pictorial or symbolic writing turns into conventional writing. That is the other boundary.

The thought life of language enters writing. Language becomes silent in writing. The thought element enters writing. As a result, writing is a kind of visible speech. The more a civilization has advanced, the less its writing reveals how the writing bubbles out of the living element in language. In the archetypal scripts, this individual and personal element could still be observed. A kind of silent, visible speech could be observed in archetypal scripts. But as humankind developed, the living element in language increasingly turned into concept and convention, that is, into something inartistic. And the more people endeavour to tie down the thinking in writing, the more writing loses its artistic element. That is why such a lack of the artistic element reaches its greatest extent in shorthand, which is quite horrible in its contrast to anything artistic.

Now we can go to the other boundary where we do not consider the thinking element in language but the will element. In speaking, the thought element, which is borrowed from the things of the external world, and the will element come together in the sound; that is, the involvement of the human being in the external world and what originates inside him are combined. What flows into writing is totally rejected. If we now study the sound in speech to turn it into eurythmy, we introduce what is externalized, rejected in writing so that we are left with what is written and nothing of the human being is any longer contained in it, it is quite separate from the human being. That is taken into eurythmy. The human being as a whole, in his totality, becomes an expression of what in speech is the will element.

This means that whereas in writing, which is also silent speech, the speech element is separated from the human being, it becomes much more intimately connected with him in eurythmy, which is wholly part of the human being. In eurythmy people do not fix what comes to expression in speech in an abstract symbol but the human being himself becomes the artistic tool of what lives in language, in poetry for example. So that language can be divided into two opposites. On the one hand there is the inartistic element in writing which is completely rejected. And if we study language inwardly through supersensory vision in such a way that we can metamorphose it into eurythmy, the human being integrates everything back into his own being. Everything that lives in terms of poetry in his will and feelings comes back to life in the movements of eurythmy. That is why what appears in eurythmy, for example as artistic movement, can be given added musical refinement. But basically eurythmy is the best expression for the true inner artistic nature of poetry.

The inner artistic nature of poetry is not the prose content of the poem but what lives in the rhythm, the beat — in short, what lives in the musical element, the element on which the words move as if on a wave. Or it is the pictorial element. Both the pictorial element in language and what lives in language, in poetry as the musical element are particularly significant in eurythmy because the human will expresses itself though the instrument of the human being. In seeing the human being in motion, which has the same effect as soul content expressed in audible speech, we have something before us which we can watch directly, which does not first need to be interpreted.

It is certainly true, that people are not yet used to eurythmy, which is why they do not understand much of it. The more people become used to it, however, the more each movement in eurythmy, each sequence of movements will be experienced quite directly as the expression of what appears in recitation, in poetry. The human being will be seen as an instrument of the soul and we will also possess the soul element — because the human being naturally lays his soul element into the eurythmy movement, the same soul element which the poet can only express incompletely in language as the inartistic thought element is also involved.

Sometimes people no longer have a real inner experience of the spoken word, people no longer hear speech but transfer that experience directly into the written word. So with regard to those things which people experience as increasingly prosaic in our civilization — if I may use that expression — which become increasingly prosaic the more they are written, with regard to those things poetry will return into human feeling, into human emotions, whenever we come to eurythmy, because with eurythmy we incorporate speech into the inner aspect of the human being, into his movements.

That is also why we cannot recite for eurythmy in the way that people recite today in our inartistic times, in our paper age. The only way to recite for eurythmy is to hear the rhythm, the beat, the musical element, so that we can experience the picture which lives in the poet, with the words in a sense only providing the vehicle for revealing the deeper aspect, the actual artistic element in the poetry. The words in themselves, not the words we hear, live in eurythmy. But this also means that the inartistic thought element vanishes and the only aspect of poetry that lives in eurythmy is the actual artistic element.

We have endeavoured recently to give shape through forms to those things which live in the feeling experience of speech. You will see in the items performed today how in serious poetry the method of the composition comes to expression, and how in humorous poems the style of the poetry is also expressed in the different style.

Eurythmy has other aspects as well, including a hygienic and therapeutic side which I do not want to go into here. It also has an educational side which has already proved its worth in the single year in which eurythmy has been an obligatory subject in the Waldorf school in Stuttgart. It has been possible to see how something quite different from mere gymnastics, which only train the body, was given to children through such ensouled gymnastics; in the latter they do not merely perform movements which are studied on a physiological basis to discover their benefit for the body, but in such ensouled gymnastics the child puts his soul into every movement he performs. That is something which an adult studying eurythmy can no longer experience, it has no great meaning for him; but in children we can see how eurythmy connects human beings with their human essence. Because the individual recovers the revelation of his soul being in what is eurythmic, one will find through eurythmy, whenever it is applied in education, that it also becomes an educational resource to develop the sense of truth. The more languages become abstract, the more untruthful they become. And the empty phrases become particularly pronounced in advanced languages because language has become separated from the human being.

In eurythmy, everything that has become separated in language is returned to the human being. In such a situation, when people have to immerse themselves in their sensations, when they make themselves into an instrument, they cannot be untruthful. And when children do eurythmy they develop a sense which counters empty phrases, they develop a sense of truth. Those are educational results which become apparent when we think about these things objectively.

For some time I have been thinking about the question how drama, for example can be expressed. At the moment we are only able to bring the epic and lyrical to expression and the essentially dramatic when it expresses a supersensory situation. You will find this presented today, drama which expresses a supersensory situation, in a piece from one of my mystery dramas. The supersensory can be adequately expressed in drama through eurythmy. But ordinary drama, performed on the basis of the sensory world, is a problem which I have set myself to tackle, and for which we will also find the eurythmy forms. As you can see, everything is still in flux.

Programme for a children's performance

Oxford, 19 August 1922

PROGRAMME

I. *Children's Performance*

Staff and Rhythmic Exercises
'I and you are we'

Energy Dance
Peace Dance
Contraction – Expansion
The Children were shouting together . . . . *A E*
The Skylark . . . . *James Hogg*
Night . . . . *William Blake*
Spring Song . . . . *Thomas Nashe*
The Camel's Hump . . . . *R. Kipling*
Three Blind Mice . . . . *Nursery Rhyme*

II.

Auftakt: Evoe   Music: Max Schuurman
Portia: The quality of mercy (The Merchant of Venice)
. . . . W. Shakespeare
'Wir wollen suchen'   Music: Max Schuurman
With a Painted Ribbon . . . . J. W. v. Goethe
Musette (Gavotte Nr. 2 aus der 3. Engl. Suite) . . . J. S. Bach
Scholastikerproblem . . . . Christian Morgenstern
Tapetenblume . . . . Christian Morgenstern
Autolycus' Song (Winter's Tale) . . . . W. Shakespeare
Under the Greenwood Tree (As you like it)
. . . . W. Shakespeare
Ingratitude: Blow, blow, thou winter wind
   (As you like it) . . . . W. Shakespeare
Tonbild . . . . Edvard Grieg
Clown's Song: When that I was
. . . . (Twelfth Night) W. Shakespeare

Supersensory physiology

It is of great importance in life that the relationships between the human being and his surroundings be properly regulated. Products provided by the outer world can be appropriately eaten and digested; but one would not be very well nourished by eating a product already partially digested by other human beings. The essential point here is that we receive the things from without in a definite form, and that they acquire their importance in life by being in turn further worked on by the human being himself.

The same holds good in higher realms as well, for example in pedagogy, the art of education. Here the important thing is to know, on the one hand, what one should learn, and on the other, in the light of what one has learned, what one should really invent in the process of teaching. If one studies education as a science consisting of all sorts of principles and formulated axioms, this means about the same thing for the art of education as it would for us to select partially digested foods for our nourishment. But if instead we acquire by study a knowledge of the human being, of the essence of the human being, and thus learn to understand him, then we take into ourselves the equivalent of what nature offers as nourishment in its realms. And in the practice of teaching there awakens in us, out of this knowledge of human nature, the educational art itself in a quite individual way. In reality this art must be invented every moment by the teacher. That is what I wished to say as a preface to today's considerations.

In instruction and education there is a curious interweaving of what is musical, the tonal element of the world through hearing, and what is pictorial in the world, which manifests itself in sight. Naturally, other sense-qualities are infused into what is imparted to us through hearing and sight, and these can under certain conditions have a secondary significance for instruction, but not the same important meaning that sight and hearing have.

Now, it is a matter of really understanding these processes right down into their corporeality. As you know, external science today distinguishes in the human being between the so-called sensory nerves, which are supposed to run from the senses to the brain, or central organ, and there transmit all perceptions and visualizations, and the motor nerves that are supposed to run from the central organ to the organs of movement, setting them in motion. You know that from the point of view of spiritual science such a differentiation is open to question. There exists no difference between the so-called sensory nerves and motor nerves. Both are of one and the same essence; and the motor nerves primarily serve no other purpose than to make us aware, at the moment when we wish to move, of the moving organ and of the process of motion itself. They have nothing to do with stimulating the will as such. Therefore we can say: we have nerves that run from our periphery more towards the centre, and we have nerves that proceed from the centre to the ends of the organs of motion; but fundamentally these are homogeneous nerve-strands. The essential point is that these nerves are interrupted, that the soul current which is carried by a nerve and which runs, for example, from a sensory nerve to the centre, is interrupted, as it were, in the centre and there must make a jump. (This is very much like the passage of an electric spark or current in a switch where the transmission is interrupted.) It is a jump to the so-called motor nerve which, however, does not thereby become anything different; on the contrary, it is exactly the same as the sensory nerve, only it has the capacity of becoming aware of the process of motion and of the moving organ itself.

But there is something that can give us an intimate insight into this whole organic process in which the psychic currents and the bodily processes interact. Let us assume, as a starting point, that we perceive a picture, that is, we are engaged in an experience that is transmitted primarily through the organ of sight—a drawing, any form in our surroundings—in short, in anything that becomes a possession of our soul through our having eyes. There we must distinguish three sharply differentiated inner activities from one another.

First we have perception as such; this perception as such actually takes place in the organ of sight. From this we must then distinguish comprehension; and in this connection we must understand that all comprehension is transmitted through the rhythmic system of the human being, not through the nervous and sensory system. Only perception is transmitted through the latter; and we comprehend a pictorial process, for instance, only through the fact that the rhythmic process, regulated by heart-lung activity, is carried on through the cerebro-spinal fluid up to the brain. In reality, comprehension is transmitted physically by the vibrations that occur in the brain and have their origin in our rhythmic system. It is through breathing that we are able to comprehend.

How mistakenly these things are generally understood by physiology today! It is believed that comprehension is connected with the human nervous system, whereas in reality it is based on the fact that the rhythmic system receives what is perceived by us and of which we form a mental picture; it then further works on it. But because the rhythmic system is linked with our comprehension, the latter comes into close relation with our feeling. Any of us who practise intimate self-perception will observe the connections that exist between comprehension and feeling itself. We must really feel the truth of what we have comprehended if we are to subscribe to it. Through the rhythmic system, a meeting takes place within us between that which derives from understanding perception and the feeling which pertains to the soul.

But then there is still a third aspect: all this must be received in such a way that the memory can retain it. In every such process, then, we have to distinguish from one another perception, comprehension and the inner processing of what was comprehended to the point at which memory can retain it. Such processing is linked with the metabolic system; and those most delicate inner metabolic processes occurring in the organism are connected with memory, with the capacity for remembering. We must pay very careful attention to these processes with which, especially as educators, we must be familiar. Just observe the difference in the memories of pale children and of those with good red complexions, or how different in regard to their power of recollection are the various races of humankind. These are all matters based on the most delicate metabolic organization and processes. If, for instance, as educators we are in a position to come to the aid of a pale child by bringing about a bit of healthy sleep for him, engendering a livelier inner stimulation of the finer metabolic processes, we can thereby greatly benefit his memory. But we can also help his memory by taking pains, as teachers, to maintain the proper balance between mere listening and active work on the part of the child. Assume that you let the child listen too much. He will arrive at perception, to be sure, and after a fashion at comprehension as well, for through his constant breathing the cerebrospinal fluid is kept in a state of activity; but the child's will would be insufficiently exerted. Now the will, as you know, is connected with the metabolism, and since mental digestion is also connected with the will as well as with the metabolism you will not be able to teach and educate well if you accustom the child too much to watching and listening, and do not have him do enough constructive work, because the will is thereby insufficiently active. You must therefore find the right balance between listening and watching on the one hand and active work on the part of the child on the other. For nothing is well retained which is not so organized in the human being that the will works into the metabolism, thus kindling the capacity for memory. These are very delicate considerations in the study of the human being that must steadily be very accurately grasped by means of spiritual science.

All of the foregoing refers to pictorial experience, to experience brought about through sight. It is different in all cases in which sound, the more or less musical element, comes into consideration. By this I do not refer only to the musical element inherent in music itself, which merely illustrates these matters especially clearly and to which it is indeed particularly applicable, but to everything connected with audibility, with what lives to a greater extent in speech and so forth. I include all of this when I speak of sound. Paradoxical as this may seem, the process here is the exact reverse of the one just described. That which in the ear comprises the sensory organization is inwardly linked in a very delicate way with all those nerves known to present-day physiology as motor nerves, but which in reality are identical with the sensory nerves; so that everything we experience as resonant sound is perceived through the nerve strands embedded in our limb organization. Everything musical, if it is to be perceived in the right way, must first penetrate deep into our whole organization—for this the nerves of the ear are appropriately organized—and must affect that region of the nerves otherwise reached only by the will. For those regions in the human organism which in the case of pictorial experiences make memory possible are the very ones that in the case of the musical, audible element give rise to perception. Thus if you search the organism for those regions that develop memory for sight perceptions, you will find in the same regions those nerves through whose agency perception itself is provided for sound perceptions. That is the reason, for example, why Schopenhauer connected music so intimately with the will. The will zones, where memory functions for sight images, are at the same time those where the perception of sound arises.

The comprehension of sound takes place also in the rhythmic system; and it is a most significant phenomenon in the human organism that things intertwine in such a particular manner. Our sight images connect with our sound perceptions and weave themselves into a common inner soul life because both are comprehended by means of the rhythmic system. Comprehension of all that we perceive comes about through the rhythmic system, sight images are perceived in the segregated head organism, and sound is perceived by the entire limb organism. Sight images flow in a current inwards towards the organism, sounds from the organism upwards.

This you must now link with what I said in the first lecture. The connection is easy to make if one feels it. Through the meeting of the two worlds in the rhythmic system there arises in our soul experience that which comprises both sound experiences and sight experiences;

and the musical — everything audible — is remembered in the same zone where the visible has its sensory and nerve organs. There at the same time lie those organs, the apparent sensory and nerve organs as external physiology calls them, which in reality are organs connected with the metabolism that affect the more delicate metabolism of the head region, through which music memories in turn come about. In the same zone in which the perception of sight images arises, music memory, the memory of everything audible, comes about as well. In the same zones in which we perceive the visible we remember the audible. In the same zones in which we remember the visible we perceive the audible; and the two cross like a lemniscate in the rhythmic system, where they dovetail and interlock.

Anyone who has ever studied music memory, so wonderful and enigmatic, though accepted as something obvious, will find how fundamentally different this music memory is from the recollection of something visible. Remembering music is based on a particular, delicate organization of the head metabolism; it is therefore, like the latter, also related in its general character to the will, and thus in turn to the metabolism; but it is located in quite a different region of the body than is the memory of sight images.

Only when you have considered these things will the whole complexity of the speech process be able to make an impression on your soul. Working outwards from within, we find in the speech process something in which first of all comprehension is expressed, because the rhythmic system is so closely linked with the speech organ. But it comes to expression in a peculiar way; and in order to make this matter wholly clear I should like to remind you of Goethe's theory of colour. Besides calling the red-yellow half of the colour world 'warm' and the blue-violet half 'cold', Goethe[13] brings colour perception and tone perception into close juxtaposition. He sees a different kind of 'sound' in the red-yellow portion of the spectrum from that in the blue-violet part, and he connects this, for instance, with the major and minor modes — that is, with certain more intimate aspects of tone experiences. This is to be found particularly in those portions of his writings on natural science which were published from the unprinted material of the Weimar Edition, and which I added in the last volume of my Kuerschner Edition [Cf. especially vol. IV, part 2, p 102 ff. of *Goethes Naturwissen-schaftliche Schriften*, edited by Rudolf Steiner (Goethe to Johann Leonhard Hoffman)]. Indeed, if we take what Goethe thus describes in his theory of colour and transfer it to the inner human being, something special results. Now, the first thing we encounter in speech is tone. Yes, tone lives in speech, but this tone is modified in a definite way. I might say it is permeated by something that dulls it in speech; and it is really not just a figurative comparison but something connected with actual processes to say that in speech the real tone is 'coloured'. The same modifica-tion that affects external colour when we perceive it 'tonally' — we do not actually perceive tone in external colour, but in a sense we hear something sounding out of every colour—the same occurs inwardly when we hear. We do not see a colour when we pronounce 'ee' or 'oo' any more than we hear tones when we see yellow or blue, but we have the same experience when we feel colour as we have in sound when we hear tone sounding out of speech. Here the worlds of sight and of sound interpenetrate each other. What we see outside in space as colours bears a quite obvious visual character, but also an intimate tone character which then enters into us, as I described at one of the previous meetings. That which proceeds as speech from within to the surface of the human being bears an obvious tone character, but also an intimate colour char- acter in sound enunciation, which in turn works its way up in a manner I have also described as applicable chiefly to the child up to his seventh year. From this you see that in the outer world it is colour and in the human inner world it is tone that remains the more manifest. And beneath the surface in the outer world there floats world music; while under the surface of sound in the inner essence of the human being there hovers and moves a mysterious astral colour element.

And now, if you properly understand speech itself— this marvellous organism detaching itself from the human being—you will feel at the same time all the vibrations of the astral body inherent in those colourful oscillations which pass directly over into speech as it sounds out of the human being. They are, of course, also active in us in other ways, but here they become peculiarly excited and con- centrated towards the larynx, receiving their impulses from the sun and moon; and all this produces a certain activity in the astral body that manifests itself externally in the movements of the larynx. And now you can consider the following possibility, at least as a picture. As you listen to speaking of any sort, observe the astral body which directly transmits its vibrations to the etheric body, making the effect of the whole process still more intimate. Now you depict all these things to produce movements founded only in the human organism. That is eurythmy, which is always executed jointly by our astral body and etheric body when we speak. There is nothing arbitrary here; it is merely a case of bringing down into visibility what otherwise constantly takes place invisibly.

Why do we do this in the present time? Because today we must do consciously what formerly we did unconsciously; for all development of the human being consists in the gradual descent of the supersensory, which at first existed only spiritually, into the sensory sphere. The Greeks, for example, really still thought with their souls; their thinking was still quite psychic. Modern human beings, especially since the middle of the fifteenth century, think with their brains. Materialism has set up one theory that is actually right when applied to the modern human being; for what the Greeks still experienced in the soul has gradually imprinted itself on the brain and has become hereditary in the brain from generation to generation. And more recently, human beings have started to think using the brain's imprints. They already think by material processes—in short, they think materialistically. That had to come. Only we must rise again; we must supplement these processes to raise ourselves to receive such revelations as come from the supersensory world. Therefore we must now add the opposite pole, the free embracing of spiritual and supersensory elements through spiritual science, to the process which imprints on the body what formerly related to the soul. But if the development of humanity is to progress, we must consciously introduce the supersensory into the sensory. We must consciously bring the human body, this body of the senses, into visible mobility in a manner that up to the present occurred invisibly, unconsciously. Thus we consciously continue along the path of the gods; we take over their work of imprinting thought upon the brain, and then we convert supersensory eurythmy into sensory eurythmy. Were we to fail in this, mankind would gradually lapse into daydreaming of the soul and become somnolent. Things would come to such a pass that although various influences would flow from the spiritual worlds into the human ego and astral body this would always take place during sleep; and on waking they would never transmit themselves to the physical organism.

When people practise eurythmy, the physical organism of those who are themselves eurythmists is turned by the eurythmy movements into a suitable organ to receive the spiritual world because the movements strive downwards out of the spiritual world. Eurythmists become organs for receiving the processes of the spiritual world by preparing their bodies for them. In the viewers of eurythmy, all eurythmy motions that relate to their astral body and ego are intensified. If you were suddenly to wake up in the night after a performance of eurythmy you would find that you had much more in you than if you had heard a sonata at an evening concert and had then awakened in the night. This effect appears to a still higher degree in eurythmy. It strengthens the soul by letting it find its way into the supersensory sphere more vividly. But here, too, a certain hygiene must govern; for if it becomes too much, the soul fidgets about in the spiritual world at night when one should sleep; and these fidgets would be the soul counterpart of physical nervousness.

You see how such things suggest an ever more real and active perception of this wondrous structure, the human organization. We become aware, on the one hand, that on the way down into the physical element nothing exists in our body that is not spiritually permeated; and on the other hand, that everything relating to the spirit and the soul aspires to a condition in which nothing psycho-spiritual should take place in the human being that is not in turn worked on in physical experience. And it is especially interesting to let these things — as I have presented them again today — sink in, and to think of them as a stimulus. If, for example, you create for yourselves vivid meditation images of everything that exists as a musical element in yourselves in the will zones of the visible; and then again, if you meditate on what is connected with memory in music, on the existence of music memories in the zones of visible representation; and if you also do that in reverse, if you connect what lies in the zones of audible representation with what lies in the memory zones of the visible — if you assemble all these phenomena and form meditation images from them, you can rest assured that a force in you will be stimulated, a profound power of ingenuity that you need when facing the child you are to educate.

The studies undertaken by education based on spiritual science have as their aim a more intimate knowledge of the human being. But if you then think about these things in meditation you cannot help affecting their continued action within yourself. If, for instance, you eat a piece of bread, you are initially concerned with a conscious process. But what then takes place, when the bread passes through the complicated process of digestion, is something over which you have little influence. Yet this process takes its course and your general life is closely bound up with it. Now, if you study the human being as we have done, you initially experience it consciously; but if afterwards you meditate upon it, an inner spiritual and soul process of digestion takes place, and that is what makes you an educator and teacher. Just as a healthy metabolic process makes an active human being out of you, so this meditative digestion of a true knowledge of the human being makes you into an educator. It is simply that you confront the child as an educator in an entirely different manner if you have lived through what results from a genuine, spiritual-scientific knowledge of the human being. In fact, that which makes educators out of us grows out of the meditative work of acquiring such a knowledge of the human being. And observations such as we have made today activate the inner soul life if we keep reawakening them within ourselves and devote even five minutes a day to them. We become so fertile in thought and feeling that what we have to give fairly bubbles forth from us. Meditate in the evening upon such knowledge of the human being, and in the morning there springs to your mind: yes, I must undertake this or that with Jack Miller. Or: that girl lacks this or that, and so forth. In short, you know what you should do in each specific case.

It is important in human life to bring about this sort of cooperation between the inner and the outer life. It does not even require very much time. Once you have inwardly mastered such things you can inwardly acquire in three seconds what will do you for a whole day of teaching when you apply it to education. Time loses its significance when it is a case of calling the supersensory to life. The spirit simply has other laws. Just as in dreams everything contracts, so all that flows from the spirit becomes extended. Just as in awaking you can have a thought which might fill weeks in terms of time, but which shoots through your mind in an immeasurably short period, so you can achieve in five minutes the whole transformation of the inner self which you need in teaching, and which then in external life makes you into something quite different from what you had been before, by thus permeating yourself through meditation with a spiritual-scientific knowledge of the human being, and provided you are at least 40 years old.

One can read about such things in the writings of people who have experienced them. It is something that must be understood; but we must also understand that what is experienced by certain individuals to an especially high degree and can then shed its light upon the whole of life, that this, on a small scale, must take place in the educator.

The educator must receive into himself the knowledge of the human being, must comprehend the knowledge of the human being by meditating, must remember the knowledge of the human being—then such memory becomes active life. It is not just common memory, but rather one that generates new inner impulses. Such memory arises from the spiritual life, which in turn flows over into our external work. That is the third stage: meditative comprehension is followed by active, creative remembering, which is at the same time a receiving of what emanates from the spiritual world. Thus we have first an acknowledgment or perception of the knowledge of the human being, then a comprehension, a meditative comprehension of such knowledge of the human being by its progressively intimate assimilation into ourselves where it is received by our whole rhythmic system, and then we have the recall of the knowledge of the human being out of the spirit. That means working educationally out of the spirit, making education an art. That must become a principle, a disposition of soul.

You must conceive of the human being in such a way that you constantly feel these three stages within yourself. And the more you are able to say to yourself: here is my outer body, here is my skin, they enclose within me the being who receives knowledge of the human being, who meditatively comprehends it, whom God has made productive through remembering it — the more you carry this feeling within you, the more you are an educator and a teacher.

3. Eurythmy therapy — the Word of the heavens is the being of man

The art of eurythmy can be a support for anthroposophical medicine when modified into eurythmy therapy. Specially trained eurythmists work together with medical doctors as Ita Wegman and Rudolf Steiner write in Fundamentals of Therapy. *Anthroposophical medicine is an extension of modern western medicine. It offers therapeutic support for the human soul and spiritual elements.*

Eurythmy therapy can intensify the dynamic relationship of the human organism to the zodiacal and planetary activities. The lecture excerpt from Cosmosophy *shows the source of speech to be, on the one hand, the echo of the life of the fixed stars, which gives rise to consonants, and on the other hand, the counteraction of planetary life, which produces the vowels. The lecture goes on to explain how the form and life of the human being arise from the creative working of these two. The anthroposophical physician considers this picture when prescribing vowels and consonants for eurythmy therapy.*

Only one exercise is included here as an example. This is the 'Light streams upwards, Weight presses downwards' movement meditation, originally presented in the context of initiation as part of a 1924 Rosicrucian lecture. This exercise has since evolved into many forms, including important applications for specific breathing disorders. The relationships of illness and therapy to spiritual development and initiation are drawn together with this exercise.

Fundamentals of therapy
(co-authored by Ita Wegman)

Within our therapeutic method, a special position is occupied by what we describe as eurythmy therapy. It is based on the eurythmy that was evolved — to begin with as a new form of art — by Rudolf Steiner out of anthroposophy.

The essential nature of the art of eurythmy has often been described by Dr Steiner, and indeed in its artistic form it has enjoyed wide recognition.

Eurythmy is represented on the stage by the human being in movement; but it is not a form of dancing. This is evident already from the fact that in eurythmy the movements of the arms and hands are above all important. Group movements enhance the whole effect, and the resulting picture on the stage gives a direct artistic impression.

All human movements are based on the inner nature of the human organization. From the same organization, in the earliest years of life, human speech proceeds. Now just as in speech the spoken sound results from the inner constitution of the human being, so, with a real knowledge of this human constitution, we can derive from the single human being — or from a group of human beings —

movements that represent genuine visible speech, or visible song. These movements are as little arbitrary as speech itself. As in a spoken word an *O* cannot be pronounced where an *I* belongs, so in eurythmy only one kind of movement gesture can appear for an *I* or for a C sharp. Eurythmy is thus a real and true manifestation of human nature, which can be evolved out of it, not indeed unconsciously like speech or song, but consciously by means of a true knowledge of the human being.

In the presentation of eurythmy we have people or groups of people in movement on the stage. The poem which is thus translated into visible speech is spoken simultaneously by a reciter. The audience hear the content of the poem and see it at the same time with their eyes. Or again, a piece of music is presented and appears at the same time as visible song in the movement gestures of the performers.

Eurythmy as a plastic art of movement constitutes a true extension of the sphere of the fine arts.

What has been discovered of an artistic nature can now be elaborated in two different directions. On the one hand it can be applied to education. In the Waldorf school in Stuttgart, which was founded by Emil Molt and placed under the direction of Rudolf Steiner, educational eurythmy is done throughout the school in addition to the physical exercises of gymnastics [this also applies to all the other Rudolf Steiner schools which have since been founded in many countries]. The fact is that in ordinary gymnastics only the dynamics and statics of the physical body are developed. In eurythmy the full human being—body, soul and spirit—goes out into the movement. The growing child feels that this is so and experiences the eurythmy exercises as a perfectly natural expression of his human nature—no less so than when in the earlier years of life he learned to speak.

The other application of eurythmy is therapeutic. The movement gestures of the pure art and of educational eurythmy, modified to arise from the sick nature of the human being in the same way as they originally arise from the healthy, give rise to a curative form of eurythmy.

The movements thus carried out act on the ill organs. We observe how the outwardly executed movement is continued inwardly with a health-giving influence on the organs, provided always that the gesture of movement is specifically adapted to the organic disease. This method of influencing the human being through movement, affecting him as it does in body, soul and spirit, works more intensely on the inner nature of the patient than any other system of therapeutic movement.

For this reason eurythmy therapy can never become an affair for amateurs. On no account must it be regarded or applied as such.

The curative eurythmist, who must be well trained in a knowledge of the human organization, may only work in collaboration with a qualified physician. All amateurish performance in this direction can only lead to ill results. It is only on the basis of a true and thorough diagnosis that eurythmy therapy exercises can be properly done.

The results of eurythmy therapy, as applied in practice, are indeed such that we may describe it as a most beneficial element within the therapeutic method explained in this book.

Consonant, vowel — nerve, blood[1]

Eurythmy, as I have often explained in these introductions to our experimental performances, should be visible speech and visible song. Now expression through sound and song, expression through speech, is located at the centre of the human experience that takes place in complete inner calm, the soul life that a person develops when he reflects on things and looks at the world with inner involvement and interest. That is when we develop our pure ideas. But such ideas are always permeated, infused by impulses of our will and mind.

Anyone who gets to know his soul life knows that even when he observes the world with his body fully at rest, when he allows the images that arise as the result of his perception to wander through his soul, expressions of the will and mind are always injected into the life of ideas, colouring and giving subtle nuances to them.

We experience a particular idea with quiet pleasure, another with quiet fear, a third with a certain reverence. We then experience wholly in the background of our soul how the will stirs — you want to possess this, take hold of something else, do a third thing.

That is the life of the soul in which the human being completely withdraws from physical manifestation and allows those things which take many different forms and movements in the world to come to inner experience, inner expression calmly within himself.

Speech and song represent the external enhancement of this whole calm inner life. We might say that in the solely reflective, thinking observation of the world the nerves play the key role in the human being and the blood only plays a role in so far as it permeates the nerves in very fine streams as carrier of the will. When we speak and sing, blood activity and nerve activity are equally involved, balancing each other out. The nerves come to expression in that they affect the breathing process and set the air in motion with the aid of the organs of speech and song. The blood comes to expression in that it is involved in the whole process of setting the air in motion through the organs of speech and song as a still undifferentiated living expression of the body. Here nerves and blood are equally involved. There is what we receive from the outside in the formation of the consonants. There is the way in which the will and the mind move inwardly in the vowel element such that the latter penetrates what is copied from the outside, adding the human element to what a person takes in from the world in expressing the consonants in speech and song. Here ideas and will meet in the soul in speech and song through feeling.

Now it is possible to have a third kind of speech, and

this third kind of speech arises when a person uses his whole organism and injects his movement and posture with what remains completely at rest during the pure observation of the world. What in speech and song is transformed from what I might call a rousing calmness into an inwardly calm movement is transformed in eurythmy wholly into posture and movement.

What lives in the consonants of speech as imitation of the external world comes to expression through the whole human being in the eurythmy forms and movements. What lives in the vowels, coming from the blood and connected with the will, is expressed in a person's posture, in the posture which is part of the movement.

When we therefore see the person or group of persons in movement on the stage in eurythmy, we always see them in a certain movement and within that movement in a certain posture. When we see movement, then it contains the consonants, which are an imitation of the external world. When we see posture, which happens in eurythmy as an expression of the vowels, then it contains what is based in the blood. Here it is the case that eurythmy is the complete opposite to what develops in a person when he is solely observing the world with inner calm. Whereas in the former the nerves are the main component and the blood as an expression of the will only plays a role in a fine flow to the extent that the will infuses the life of the nerves, it is the case in eurythmy that the key element is what the body does in terms of movement and posture in doing all these things on the basis of the will based in the blood. Here it is the case that in eurythmy it is primarily the blood organism that is active and the nerves to the extent that they serve the blood circulation, that is, the inner rhythm, the inner-most rhythm of the human being.

And so one can have working on one jointly the inner rhythm of the human organism transformed into move-ment and posture, arising from the will element of the soul, and that aspect which lies somewhat higher and is closer to the human being as observer: speech and song.

When there is recitation for the eurythmy movement, we cannot recite in the way that is popular in today's inartistic times, where the prose content of the poem is merely emphasized. But the creation of the sound must be infused with what is hidden eurythmy, the rhythm of the sound, the beat as well as the melody and harmony; the harmony of the sound, the harmony of the sound creation must be infused in this way.

If we see eurythmy and declamation or recitation orchestrally together in this way, then we should become aware of what a person always experiences when he experiences himself through his soul. Because the soul is intimately connected with the body, the human being wishes to copy in the body what he experiences inwardly in the soul. The soul lives in the human organism down to the fingertips and it can copy everything that lives in it physically in space. In speaking and singing, it restricts to the chest organism what could otherwise be expressed in the whole human being, in movement and posture. And because the chest organism has particular organs asso- ciated with what would otherwise be the total movement and total posture in the human being, the same thing as posture and movement is expressed in human speech and song, but in the latter case is transformed into the invisible movement of the air while in the human being himself it only comes to expression through the soul in tone and sound. And thus the only thing which is suppressed in what you see here as the depiction of eurythmy is the observing human being. While the human being is revealed externally in his mind, for which the chest organs are used, and in his whole shape, for which the will organs, organs of movement, are used, the observing human being is absent on the stage and in declamation and recitation.

In fact, the viewer or the listener is the observing human being. The latter opens himself to what is happening on the stage or at the lectern. He takes in what happens there, in other words, he becomes involved in that most perfect of instruments which the eurythmist uses: the whole of the human organism. He sees and looks at the human being to the extent that a person is a being that reveals himself externally. And thus the manifestation of the human being in the external world becomes internalized through observation itself.

Whereas we are dealing with separate instruments in the other arts and the artist only utilizes such separate instruments, the human being himself becomes an instrument in eurythmy. Hence the microcosm, this small world, is presented to the human being in eurythmy and the viewer can say to himself: the internal cannot become the content of art but only what is revealed externally, because art must be seen and perceived.

But everything that the human being can develop externally is presented to the inner life of the viewer. Although the audience has to be asked for its indulgence every time that such an experiment in eurythmy is presented, because all of it is still in the beginning stages if we consider what it can be in the future, we can nevertheless say that it will present to the inward nature of soul and spirit in the most delicate motions and revelations what has an external effect in the human soul and spirit being.

And in this way eurythmy will present soul and spirit in fullest concentration for the viewer to watch. And that is basically the highest ideal of all art. That is why we hope that this art in particular will find its place as a fully justified younger art next to the fully justified older arts as an addition to everything else: the poetic, rhythmical, musical, sculptural and architectural, and in synthesis of them all. We may hope for that if we consider what eurythmy uses as its means of expression — the human being as he is revealed externally — and to what it appeals: to that element in the human being which has the fullest and most complete interest in human nature to the extent that the latter is a microcosmic expression, a revelation of the greater world, the macrocosm.

Cosmosophy — the life of the senses and the life of movement

Yesterday I spoke of the relationship of the human form in its twelve aspects to the fixed stars. Today I have tried to show you how the new science of anthroposophy is in agreement with the instinctive wisdom of old in saying that the different levels of human life are connected with the life of the planets in the cosmos. Depending on the position of the earth in relation to the different members of the planetary system and the sun at its centre, life is modified in many different ways. Life is made to die, it is preserved and made creative in the upper human being. It is reduced in the lower human being so that physical matter and energies can be taken up from the earth. Human beings simply take the earth's power of repulsion, make it their own and in this way develop the power that is in their own organs, and so on.

We see, then, that human life, too, comes from the cosmos. Looking up to the fixed stars, we see the zodiac as representing the principles that give rise to the human form. Observing the movements of the planets, we find the explanation for the different levels of human life. We look to Saturn for the life of the senses, to Jupiter for the life of the nerves, to Mars for the life of breathing, which is active in images.

Let us take a special look at this life of breathing. I told you that the images are received from the cosmos: form. The movements experienced in the zodiac stream inwards as images of our internal organs. Between birth and death, human beings are on earth, however, and the lower aspect acts into the upper, with the result that everything has its polar opposite. The images enter into us and become suffused with matter, otherwise we would have no internal organs. But there is also always a counter-process. So we are able to say that when we breathe the images are pushed inwards, the image of the kidney for example.

Matter then fills this out [red]; but the opposite also happens, this time in an upward direction, with the images thrown back, as it were, like an echo. But do not think of this as a once-only event. The organs exist, having been developed in the early stages of earth existence; but the counter-action may go on all the time. The role played by the soul element in this will be considered tomorrow.

Consider each on its own, therefore. You assimilate the images of your internal organs with the life process. Then comes the counter-action, in which the echoes of those images rise up again, as does the zodiac, especially with the life of breathing in it. Well, just think of your ears, and there you have the counter-process. These images are created and go out into the air—they are the vowels and consonants! The vowels come more from the planets, the consonants from the zodiac. The counter-process to the images coming in is reflected in speech. Consonants and vowels enter into us to be the foundation for our organs. Anything that tends towards form inside us comes essentially from the zodiac, anything that tends towards life comes essentially from the planets. If the counter-action relates more to life, we produce vowels; if it relates more to form, we produce consonants. All this is to some extent connected with breathing, and we can see that quite clearly in speech.

You see, it is not really a good idea to try to understand the human being by putting him on the dissecting table and investigating what lies beneath the skin. The result of this is no better than if someone were to take a magnetic needle and ignore the fact that the earth itself is a large magnet, making one end point north and the other south. If anyone were to insist on producing a theory that the magnetic needle takes that position of its own accord, ignoring the fact that the forces of the earth give it that particular direction, it would be just like anatomists and physiologists trying to understand the human being on the basis of what is to be found beneath the skin. You cannot understand the human being on the basis of what lies beneath the skin. All the people who seek to explain speech and language on the basis of what lies inside the human being are working on the same level as the explanation that a magnetic needle points north of its own accord. The truth is that human beings take in form from the life of the fixed stars and reproduce this as an echo, which gives rise to the consonants. They take in the movements of planetary life, which influence their own life. The life of breathing in particular creates images of all this. The counter-action then produces the vowels. Human speech can only be understood if consonants are seen in relation to the constellations of fixed stars and vowels in relation to planetary conjunctions and opposi-tions. Thus human speech and language derives from the whole cosmos.

The sun, here [horizontal line in diagram below], marks the middle. Take the three upper principles and you have

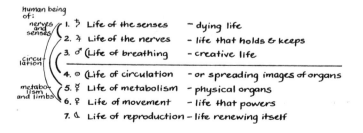

the upper human being. Take the three lower principles and you have the lower human being. The reproductive life then gives rise to a new human being.

Take the breathing and circulation. The latter essentially reflects the planetary movements. Our blood circulation is basically no more than an image of planetary life. We may thus also say that the vowels come from the circulation and the consonants from the breathing. And now we get another strange relationship. We can relate the metabolism to the nerves and movement to the senses. The life of the senses, however, relates to the movements of Saturn, which may be said to be closest to the zodiac, just as human beings present themselves most clearly to the outside world in their movement. If we want to show how human beings reflect the secrets of the cosmos, we have on the one hand the senses and on the other hand movement and this gives us— eurythmy. Eurythmy is the direct image of the relationship human beings have to the cosmic periphery. I just wanted to mention this briefly.

My purpose today has been to show you how the human being relates to the cosmos with regard to life. Yesterday it was my purpose to show the relationship of the human being to the cosmos with regard to form. Tomorrow we will consider the third aspect of the relationship between the human being and the cosmos— the soul. After considering the human soul in relation to the life of the cosmos we will have the three aspects of form, life and soul.

Light and weight

We have seen how the knowledge that human beings used to acquire in ancient days by means of instinctive clairvoyance gradually faded away into a kind of evening twilight. It is actually quite difficult to find any trace of that ancient wisdom in modern times, particularly since the eighteenth century, for all that is now left to us—or rather, I should say, what has recently come in its place—is the external observation of nature, and logic. And neither with external observation of nature nor with the mere sequence of abstract logical thoughts can people build a bridge to reach reality. Much of the ancient wisdom nevertheless maintained a sort of existence in traditional form right on into modern times, even as late as the middle of the nineteenth century. And in order that we may orientate ourselves correctly with regard to the important subjects with which we shall have to deal, I should like today to tell you about some of the ideas that were still to be found in the first half of the nineteenth century as survivors of the ancient wisdom, in order that you may see how in a time that does not lie so very far back there were people whose whole manner of thinking was entirely different from what it is today. As I said, it is exceedingly difficult to arrive at these things, for it is single individuals, living alone, or having around them at best a small circle of pupils, who preserved the ancient wisdom in strict secrecy—and often without themselves understanding it in all its profundity. And a similar picture applies to the conditions that prevailed in still earlier times, for it is quite certain that the two characters familiar to you under the names of Faust[2] and Paracelsus[3] encountered in the course of their wanderings solitary individuals of this kind—cave-dwellers of the soul one might call them—and learned a great deal from them, which they afterwards developed and elaborated through an inner faculty that was, in their case too, of a rather instinctive nature.

However, what I am now going to relate to you belongs to a much later period; it will illustrate for you how things were in the early decades of the nineteenth century. Once more we find a little group—call it a school if you will—a solitary school somewhere in central Europe. There, in this quite small circle, was to be found a deep and penetrating teaching concerning the human being. A long time ago, I became aware—on a spiritual path—that at a certain place in central Europe there existed such a small company of people who had knowledge. As I have said, I learned about it on a spiritual path. I was not able at that time to make observations in the physical world, for I was not then in the physical world; but on a spiritual path it became known to me that a little company of this kind existed.

I would not, however, speak about what was taught within this little company, had not the essence of what was hidden in it subsequently again disclosed itself to research made independently through spiritual science; I would not speak of it, had I not myself found this knowledge again. For it is precisely in its rediscovery that one obtains the right attitude to the wisdom that has survived from ancient times, a wisdom that is truly overpowering in its greatness. For this little company of which I speak, a tradition goes right back in history, back through the whole of the Middle Ages into the times of antiquity that I was describing to you in the lectures given at the Christmas meeting,[4] into the age of Aristotle.[5] The tradition does not, however, come directly from Greece; it comes from Asia, whither it was brought from Macedonia by Alexander the Great.[6]

Within this little company a deep and strikingly exact teaching was given concerning the human being, especially with regard to two human faculties. We can see there a spiritual scientist—for he may truly be so called— who is a highly developed master, instructing his pupils. The ancient symbols by which he teaches them consist in certain geometrical forms—say, for example, a form such as this [diagram on next page], and at the points would generally be found some words in Hebrew. At first sight one can make nothing whatever of such symbols. And the pupils of this master would have known through the instruction they received that what, for example, Eliphas Levi[7] gives later on is in reality no more than talking round the subject, for these pupils were still able to learn how the true meaning of such symbols is only arrived at when they are rediscovered in the nature and being of the human being himself.

There was in particular one symbol that played a significant part in this little group of seekers. You have the
symbol before you when you draw apart this 'Solomon's
Key'[8] so that one triangle comes down and the other
rises [diagram]. The symbol thus obtained played, as I
said, a significant part within this little community or
school, and continued to do so even as late as the nineteenth century.

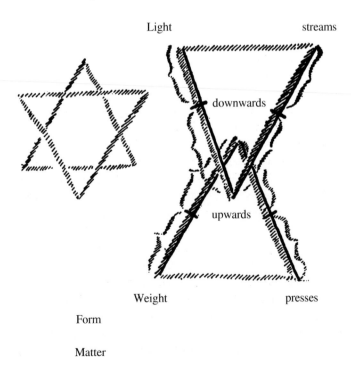

Light   streams

downwards

upwards

Weight   presses

Form

Matter

The master would then get the pupils to assume a certain attitude with their physical bodies. The body itself had to 'draw' this symbol. He made them stand with their feet far apart, and their arms stretched out above. Then, by lengthening the lines of the arms downwards and the lines of the legs upwards, these four lines [darker in the diagram] came to view in the human organism itself. A line was then drawn to unite the feet, and another to unite the hands above; and these two joining lines had to be felt as lines of force. The pupil became conscious that they do really exist; it became clear to him that currents, not unlike electromagnetic currents, pass from the left fingertips to the right fingertips, and again from the left foot to the right. So that in actual fact the human organism itself writes into space these two intersecting triangles.

The pupil had then to learn to feel the content of the words 'Light streams upwards, Weight bears downwards'. He had to experience this in deep meditation, standing in the attitude I have described. In this way he gradually came to the point where the teacher was able to say to him: 'Now you are about to experience something that was practised over and over again in the ancient mysteries.' And the pupil did then actually achieve this further experience, namely, that he could feel the very marrow within the bones of his limbs [see dark lines in diagram].

You will be able to come a little nearer to an understanding of such experiences if you recall something I said to you yesterday. I told you then, in another connection, that if a person continues to think so abstractly as has by now become the custom, if he goes on living entirely in abstract thoughts, he will externalize himself, he will become something altogether external. The exact opposite happens when, in this way, the human being achieves a consciousness of the interior of the bones.

Let me tell you something else that will help you to a clearer understanding of the matter. Paradoxical as it may sound, it is nevertheless true that a book such as my *Philosophy of Freedom*[9] cannot be grasped by logic alone, it needs the whole human being. You will in fact fail to understand what is said in the book about thinking, unless you know that the human being experiences thought by means of an inner experience of his skeleton. A person does not really think with his brain; when he thinks in sharply defined thoughts, he thinks with his skeleton. When, however, as is the case in the *Philosophy of Freedom*, thought becomes concrete, becomes real, then it goes over into the whole human being.

The pupils of this master went even further. They learned to feel the actual inside of the bones, and that enabled them to experience a last example of what was practised in many different ways in the ancient mystery schools: they learned to experience symbols by turning their own organism into a symbol. Only so can symbols be truly experienced! Explanation and interpretation of symbols is quite nonsensical; so too is all theorizing about them — utter nonsense. One has to make them, one has to experience them. It is the same with symbols as it is with fables and legends and fairy tales; one has to identify oneself with them. There is always something in the human being through which he can enter into all the figures of the fairy tale, through which he can make himself one with the fairy tale. And so it is with these genuine symbols of ancient times which come originally from spiritual knowledge. I have, as you see, written the words in your own language [see diagram]. There is very little sense in writing on the diagram Hebrew words that are no longer understood; for then the person who reads them will not be inwardly quickened, will have no inward experience of the symbol; on the contrary, he will be cramped by it, will feel as though his bones are being broken. And that is also what really happens — spiritually of course — when one takes seriously such writings as those of Eliphas Levi.

These pupils, then, learned to experience the inside of their skeletal system. But, my dear friends, when you begin to experience the inside of your bones, you are no longer really in the body! If you hold your finger a few inches in front of your nose, then what you are holding there is not in you; just as little is what you experience within your bones really in you. You go inwards, it is true; nevertheless, you go out of yourself. And this going out of oneself, this going to the gods, this going to the spiritual world, is what the pupils of that solitary school learned to grasp and understand. For they learned to know the lines the gods had drawn into the world, the lines that had been drawn by the gods to establish and found the world. They discovered — in one direction, namely, through the human being — the path to the gods.

The healing process

I have now presented the essentials of what I wanted to tell you about our anthroposophically-based methodological efforts and the path linking the outer natural world and the interior of the human body. In conclusion, I would like to draw your attention to the great significance of the manner in which substances that relieve the human body of disease processes are administered. If it is true that the human being is a threefold being with a sensory and nervous system, a rhythmical system, and a metabolic and limb system, then healing too can be subdivided into three processes. The first includes all medications that are administered orally and find their way into the body through digestion. Through injection, we attempt to incorporate healing functions into the rhythmic organism. The third method of healing is through baths, which work from outside and affect the sensory and nervous process. Although baths are a rather crude means of working from outside, their effects do involve a lower level of perceptual activity.

Let us consider these three methods of administration with regard to phosphorus. Phosphorus, when mixed with other substances, processed by chemical or other means and administered orally, promotes fluid absorption into the human organism. Suppose we have to relieve the human body of disease symptoms in which the fluid element exceeds its proper bounds, such as certain inflammations or nosebleeds, to use trivial examples. In such cases, orally administered phosphorus relieves the astral organism and the 'I' of a pathological fluid function. Preparing and administering an appropriate dose of phosphorus by injection relieves the organism of symptoms related to abnormal circulation. Phosphorus injections can have extremely beneficial effects on such conditions as accelerated respiration, intensified cardiac activity or excessive rhythmical gall secretion, to list the most obvious. On the psychological side, when brain function causes ideas to overflow involuntarily, so that patients cannot restrain their thoughts and their words bubble over, baths containing dissolved phosphorus will slow down their train of thought. These specific examples could be multiplied a hundredfold. There are three basic ways of influencing the human body. It is simply a question of how to bring about the desired effect.

Another therapeutic approach entails directly involving patients in universal movements that act on the metabolic system from outside. Eurythmy therapy does this successfully. Eurythmy is something like spiritual gymnastics, but it can be elevated to the level of an art. Frau Steiner has already directed artistic eurythmy performances throughout central and northern Europe, including presentations here in The Hague some time ago. In eurythmy, we see an artistic translation of human speech into human movement. If you think of the scientific details known today about the relationship between hand and arm activity and the human speech apparatus, namely, that the speech centre in right-handed people is located on the left side of the brain, while the opposite is true of left-handed people, anthroposophy's conclusion that all human speech is related to movement may no longer seem questionable.

Consonant sounds, especially palatal consonants, show us how our feet and legs move. When we follow our arm movements, we can see that they too are translated into movements of the air in speech. Linking speech as a whole to the movements of an individual or a group results in artistic eurythmy. Its gestures originate in the entire human being of body, soul and spirit, while the gestures of ordinary gymnastics arise from the physiological constitution of the physical body.

However, appropriate movements taken from artistic eurythmy can also be transformed and developed to be performed by patients in a therapeutic context. We have worked out an entire system of eurythmy therapy in our Arlesheim clinic. When eurythmy therapy is implemented consistently, it works back on the human body and supports internal healing processes—the three types I mentioned—in an exceptionally fruitful way. Eurythmy therapy works because the normal dynamic process that results when a person walks, runs, and so on, also works back on internal degenerative and regenerative processes. Because this interaction is highly specific, one set of eurythmy therapy gestures will stimulate degenerative processes that are not taking place in the right way, while a different set of gestures will counteract excessive degenerative processes.

Such a therapeutic approach depends entirely on understanding the human being, whether healthy or ill, as a being of body, soul and spirit. Once we have understood this, we will be able to read the meaning of a person's health or illness, and the appropriate treatment becomes evident in what we see.

These are our modest attempts at rational therapy. I know that many objections will be raised to such therapy and that it will be seen as paradoxical or worse by all those who have expended a great deal of energy on mastering officially sanctioned treatments. This is not a new situation, however. I can assure you that I would be more comfortable if I did not have to speak on this subject, because I am personally familiar with all the possible objections that result from habitual ways of thinking. However, the belief that there is a need to introduce something new into our culture is sufficient reason to speak about it. I ask you to acknowledge my responsibility in this regard and to accept my sincere thanks for your attention to my explanations, which were limited to brief indications by the two hours we had available.

4. Silent soul: Speaking soul. Eurythmy as a performing art

Johann Wolfgang von Goethe wrote both scientific and poetic treatises on the metamorphosis of plants. His thesis may be expressed by 'everything is leaf', implying that the archetype of the whole can always be found in the smallest part. Rudolf Steiner says in the first extract of this section that Goethe's teaching of metamorphosis forms the basis of eurythmy.

This first selection is unique in that it contains a rare reference to the nature of speech eurythmy's silent introductions and conclusions (Vortakt and Nachtakt), called here 'evolutions'. An example of such a silent form is included.

Eurythmy as a performing art requires the foundation of a full artistic eurythmy training – Steiner here recommends five years – as well as an additional training in stagecraft. Stagecraft includes the selection of pieces for specific programmes, choreography, costumes, colour and lighting. Light eurythmy is the common voice between the lit space and the colours of the dresses and veils. This section also has a few words for actors on the value of eurythmy for their profession.

Metamorphosis

You will perhaps allow me to say just a few short words before our attempt to give a performance of eurythmy. It is not my purpose to try to explain the content of this performance for the reason that all that is of the nature of art must speak for itself. An explanation of any kind is not in itself 'artistic' and would consequently be out of place here. It is, however, necessary to say a few words because what we here call the art of eurythmy is derived from sources hitherto unfamiliar to the world of art, and makes use of an artistic language whose forms are likewise rather unusual.

Eurythmy is the art of movement in space carried out by individuals and groups of individuals in reciprocal relationships and positions. These movements are not mere gestures, nor are they mime. Eurythmy as we here perform it cannot therefore be regarded as anything in the nature of dance; it is a new art, having as its instrument the human being himself, and its movements are absolutely in accordance with its laws. The movements that are made in the larynx and the other organs of speech when a person expresses himself in sound have been studied by a kind of perception which is at the same time 'sensory' and yet 'supersensory' — if I may use an expression from Goethe. But in audible speech those inner movements or, better, those underlying principles of movement which it is the function of the larynx and the other organs of speech to bring to expression are arrested as they arise and are transformed into finer vibratory movements which by means of the air carry the sound so that it can be heard. In eurythmy, then, a process as yet within the human organs of speech is interpreted by one individual or by groups of individuals. Goethe's teaching of metamorphosis forms the basis of this art. Everything that we do here is founded on Goetheanism and the art of eurythmy is just one aspect of it.

Goethe developed his teaching of metamorphosis on the basis of his universal world conception. The following rather abstract remarks about the simple way in which Goethe applied this teaching of the metamorphosis of plants are not made with the purpose of evolving a theory, but only of making myself clear.

In principle, Goethe sees a complete plant in each single leaf, so that a plant as a unit originates from the right development of what lies as idea within each single leaf. The whole plant is, in principle, an elaborated leaf, and each individual leaf is a primitive plant. What Goethe worked out with regard to organic metamorphosis — for he expanded the range of his conception to cover all organisms — can be applied to organic functions and development and then transformed into art. So that if we turn what exists in principle and as idea in a single group of organs — such as the larynx and other organs of speech — into movements carried out by a person, making that person or a group of people into a living larynx in movement, as it were, we get visible speech. And what lies at the basis of eurythmy is such visible speech.

It is obvious, of course, that there will be opposition to art of this nature, employing as it does methods that are unfamiliar. But such opposition will disappear in the course of time. The gestures are not accidental in eurythmy; there is no mere chance connection between

Speech Eurythmy

some movement of the arms, for instance, and a certain emotion of the soul. Just as a definite shade of tone in speech corresponds to a soul process, and vice versa, you find in eurythmy a logical sequence of movements; that which comes to expression in speech, song, music is represented in eurythmy by means of a different artistic medium, by a different form of speech. Hence, as you will see, eurythmy can be accompanied by music, for that which in music is expressed in tone is expressed by the movements of a person. This visible speech of eurythmy can also be accompanied by audible speech, such as recitation or declamation. The poem is recited and the real artistic content of it is translated into eurythmy — into visible speech. In this way we can see how eurythmy in this somewhat inartistic age may be able to develop a true artistic understanding and rendering of recitation and declamation.

With reference to recitation and declamation it is the verbal content of the poem which is considered specially important today. But the real artistic value of poetry is not determined by this verbal content so much as by the plastic and figurative or musical element to be found in it. When, therefore, recitation or declamation accompanies eurythmy, special care must be taken that they bring out the artistic element, the rhythm, the metre and the inner form of the language used. In that way we shall get back to an understanding of the art of recitation as it existed in ages that were truly artistic. It is interesting in this connection to remember that when Goethe studied his iambic[1] dramas with the actors he always used a baton as if he were conducting music, showing that he attached more importance to the iambic formation of his verses than to their verbal content. Eurythmy will also have an influence upon recitation because the art of recitation must accompany that which forms the artistic basis of eurythmy.

As the months have gone by we have developed the subject. At first we expressed the poetic content by the visible speech of eurythmy while the recitation itself was going on. Now we are trying to impart the essential content of a poem, for instance, by means of evolutions that precede and follow it, so that the visible but unaccompanied language of eurythmy can also be displayed to advantage by itself.

That, briefly, is the artistic side of the question, and it represents one aspect of eurythmy as we practise it. The other is the educational element. Eurythmy, besides being of the nature of art, is a kind of spiritualized gymnastics. As such, it is used in the Waldorf school which was founded in Stuttgart by Emil Molt and organized and directed by me. Eurythmy, as well as gymnastics, has been introduced there as a compulsory subject in all the classes. It is true to say that in ages more artistically unbiased than ours, there will be a quite different way of judging gymnastics. Just recently a famous modern physiologist came here, heard what I said as an introduction to eurythmy and also saw the performance. His opinion was that from a physiological point of view ordinary gymnastics was not

Silent introduction of Lynceus, the night watchman in Goethe's Faust
*(Part II, Act V), who is about to speak about the beauty of nature and the
cruelty of man.*

a method of education at all, but so much barbarism. Remember, it is not I who say that, but a modern physiologist whose name people respect tremendously. I myself do not go nearly so far; I say that gymnastics is carried out according to physical laws built up merely on a physiological basis, whereas when a child is allowed to carry out the movements of eurythmy, all of which are full of meaning, then the whole of its being—body, soul and spirit—is affected and not the body only. After a year of experience in the Waldorf school, we have already been able to see the delight with which the children have made this art of eurythmy their own. They really feel that these movements proceed from the human constitution itself. The natural joy of a child learning to speak may be compared with that of children between the ages of 7 and 15 who are beginning to practise these eurythmy movements. They find that the human element in them is being guided into a correct course. Out of the four hundred children in the Waldorf school there were at the very most two or three who did not enter into the thing as joyfully as was the case with all the others; the number of children who for some fundamental reason took to eurythmy with difficulty was quite negligible, the remainder taking the very greatest delight in their eurythmy lessons. I say without hesitation that eurythmy develops something in children that is really needed; and that is initiative of soul and of will, which gymnastics, as such, cannot do.

We ask everybody to remember that we ourselves are the most severe critics of what we are attempting to do.

Eurythmy is still at its most elementary stage. But while we realize that we are only attempting to make a beginning, we can affirm that through further development brought about either by ourselves or by others, eurythmy will become ever more perfect, and will one day take up its rightful position as a young sister art among the older and fully established ones.

I U A drawing

Mrs Fels: In school, the children have to be allowed to quieten down after the lesson. Does the same apply to the students of the eurythmy school? Some students asked to do one of the weekly verses (from the Calendar of the Soul)[2] *or something similar.*

Dr. Steiner: It is not recommended to start with the weekly verse since all kinds of different people are accepted on the courses not all of whom are even members of the Society.[3] That creates a certain atmosphere which may quickly lead to ridicule.

In other schools it is common to start the day with a prayer. Do you think we should do that? It is not really appropriate. If anything, you should proceed by saying that it is good to start with a general rhythm and then close with it at the end. You can compose a round-dance which goes such that the people take their positions and make the figure and then do the same at the end. In other words, start and finish with it, always with the same music. It could be an extended, melodious chord; that would be very nice. You can also add: *i, u, a*; an extended chord or have them start with *i, u, a*; have them do it in a circle a few times.

Archival photo. Chorus from a Greek drama. Left to right: Astrid von Wageningen-Schenkel, Maria Jenny-Schuster, Elena Zuccoli, Marie Savitch, Lea van der Pals, Ida Schweigler-Ritter, Emica Mohr-Senft.

Costumes and colour

In the *e* sound we have the expression of being affected by something and of standing up against it. This is expressed in the green colour. Green is obtained by mixing together yellow and blue, thus by a combination of a light and a dark colour. Here we have the *e* expressed directly through the colour itself. You grow into the feeling of this gesture when you associate it with this colour. It is quite impossible to enter into these things with our reason; they can only be felt and experienced inwardly. For our purposes, however, we will assume that we have absorbed all this, and have come so far as to recognize that the mood of any particular sound is really represented by the corresponding eurythmy figure. Let us take the mood of the *e* sound. We will gradually discover for ourselves that whole poems are really permeated throughout with the *e* mood. No matter how many other vowels occur in such a poem, it nevertheless has the *e* mood running right through it. Take, for example, a poem or any text which is to be expressed in eurythmy in which, let us say, there continually occurs the feeling of being unpleasantly affected by something, but at the same time a certain resistance against what is affecting us in this way. When a poem has such a mood running through it, we should do well to choose these colours [*e* figure] for the dress and veil. The important thing is to learn to associate definite colours with each particular sound; then we shall gradually reach the point at which we are able to select dresses and veils suitable to a poem as a whole.

Lighting and costume indications

BACH, Johann Sebastian

Sarabande
from the 2nd Cello Suite in D minor

		Bar
1.	above blue green	1–2
	below red green	

2. above red yellow   3–6
   below red green

3. above red   7–13
   below red green

4. above red   14–22
   below blue green

5. above red blue   23–28
   below blue green

blue costume
pale red veil

Brouwer[4]
26 November 1923

Light eurythmy

Dornach, 30 September 1922
Eurythmy is thus a truly visible speech that can be created just as artistically as music or the poetic expression of recitation or declamation, only in this case for the eye and not for the ear. Then we endeavour to adapt the whole stage setting to the eurythmy staging. And those in the audience who have seen earlier performances of eurythmy will note that we have been attempting for some time to design the

lighting—both the lighting of the space and the lighting coordinated with the colour of the costumes and veils—to accord with eurythmy. So that in a certain sense we have a flood of light, either internally or generally in motion, which in turn represents visible speech.

Dornach, 2 April 1923

We have recently introduced the element of light and colour into eurythmy. Let me say that what appears on the stage as the movement of a person or a group of people comes from the human soul, the human spirit. But the human soul element is always connected with the elemental part of the external world. And what happens on the stage in the images produced by the movement of people can be harmonized in that it is harmoniously continued and developed in what then floods the stage as colour and light effects—effects which on the one hand are coordinated with the costumes of the eurythmists and on the other hand in their sequence produce what I might describe as a musical element born out of sound. So the lighting of the stage can also be treated eurythmically. The stage setting for eurythmy is still imperfect today but it will become more and more perfected.

Dornach, 11 May 1924

For some time now we have endeavoured to introduce a eurythmy element with increasing perfection into the sequence of lighting on the stage, which is then a continuation of what occurs in the movement of the people or

Rudolf Steiner and Marie Steiner (seated, centre) with the Eurythmy Group in Dornach, 1921.

groups of people. That is why it must not be seen as something of superficial importance, but as something artistic. We can already introduce things to the staging which must gradually be introduced to a greater degree.

Thus when it grows light on the stage during the recitation and presentation of a poem in eurythmy, then this change in the lighting does not occur because it says in the poem that the sun is shining, but because something bright occurs at this point in the language.

We are, however, aware that we are still in the beginning stages. After all, I only recently attempted to move tone eurythmy forward a little by giving a course on tone eurythmy here in the School of Spiritual Science,[5] a special course on tone eurythmy. We are, as I said, still in the early stages and are our severest critics in this respect.

The eurythmy training

Friday, 30 March 1923

A teacher: In the other upper grades, there are many who want to go into eurythmy.

Dr Steiner: Then they should not take the final examination. When the eurythmy school is halfway established, we will have to develop eurythmy more completely [see faculty meeting of 12 June 1920]. It cannot remain the way it is now, but will have to be more completely developed.

When someone wants to become a ballet dancer, they must undergo training for seven years. We also need to have some supplementary subjects. In time, it will be absolutely necessary to have a genuinely human education there. Related arts such as dance and mime will also have to be taught. If the eurythmy school is to be successful, we must develop it further. Such training will most certainly need five years. We cannot afford to just wildly produce eurythmists. Those who will later become teachers certainly need to have a complete education. They need to know something about the human being also. They will need an education in literary history, for example. Slowly, we will have to develop a proper curriculum.[6]

The question now is whether we could free those who are to become eurythmists from those classes they do not want to take. They could then go over to the eurythmy school and learn there.

It would be best if we did not split the curriculum at the Waldorf school with eurythmy. We would have to do things such that when there is a split those who are moving on would not take the final examination. That is, those who want to have further education in art could not take Latin and Greek.

What the actor learns from eurythmy

And now I have something to say on more general lines as regards a school of dramatic art. It is of great importance that an actor should have a good knowledge of eurythmy. Not in order to perform it, for eurythmy is an art that is performed on the stage on its own account. But all the other arts have to make their contribution to the full training of an actor, and so too eurythmy. I do not mean that an actor should let his acting run on here and there into eurythmy. The result would be most inartistic. Eurythmy can only be artistic when it is allowed to work in its own way, that is, to the accompaniment of recitation or music. We must have a feeling for what it is in eurythmy that makes it an art. Eurythmy provides what cannot come to expression in music alone or in recitation alone; it takes these further, continues them. No one could feel it to be true eurythmy if done to the accompaniment of singing. In singing, music has flowed over into speech. Eurythmy would merely disrupt the singing, and singing would do the same to eurythmy. Eurythmy can be accompanied by recitation, which itself has nothing to do with bodily movement; for in recitation gesture has become inward. Eurythmy can also be accompanied by instrumental music. But not by singing, if one wants to let eurythmy work in a way that corresponds to its true ideal.

Not directly, therefore, but indirectly eurythmy can be of the very greatest importance for the actor. For what have we in eurythmy? In eurythmy we have the full, the microcosmic gesture for vowels and consonants. *I* [arm stretched straight out]; a still more intensely pointed *I* [fingers also stretched]. And now try to continue inwards the feeling you have in making the eurythmy for *I*. I do not mean merely the feeling of having your arm and hand in that position; the *I* lies in the feeling that is experienced in the muscle. Try to keep hold of this feeling within you; experience it as though a sword were being thrust straight down into your body. And now, continuing this feeling still further, try to intone *I*. Then the correct nuance for your *I* will come to you from eurythmy; your *I*, as you speak it, will have the necessary purity. And it will be the same with the other vowels and consonants. Continue their eurythmy inwards; fill yourself with the spirit of the eurythmic form, with its mirrored reflection and, while still feeling the form there within you, intone the sound. In this way you will come to speak your vowels and consonants in all purity. So much for advice of a more general kind concerning your training.

If you continue to keep all these things in mind, you will gradually acquire a true understanding for what is essential in speech. For it is not enough for an actor to know his part. He must of course do that; but what matters above all is that he should have the right thoughts and feelings concerning his vocation. Otherwise he cannot really be an actor. No one can be an artist in any sphere who fails to have a true and worthy conception of his art.

By entering with your whole heart into such a training as I have indicated here, you will come to have a pure — let me say, a religious — understanding of what speaking really is, and not only with regard to speaking but also the mime and gestures that are connected with it. And that is what is needed. For such a conception of speech will, more than anything else, give you a strong and clear feeling of the place of the human being in the universe. Gradually you will come to appreciate the human being's true dignity and value, seeing how he stands at the very centre of the cosmos. Look at the animals. They too make sounds. Think of the lion's roar, of the lowing of the cow, or of the bleating of sheep and goats. The sounds produced by these animals have the character of vowels. They are expressing what lies within them — as do all the animals that make a sound in this manner. And then, as you go about the world of nature, you will also hear quite different sounds, such as for example the sounds that are made by cicadas and other insects, where the sound is produced by the movements of certain limbs or organs. There you have sounds that show a decided consonantal character. And then at last you come to that wonderful development of sound that means so much to human beings — the song of the birds! In the singing of birds you have music. So that while you hear vowels from the higher and consonants from the lower animals, the birds give you the possibility to hear music in the animal world. But now what about that sound you hear when you go out into the country and listen to the cicadas or other insects? Go close up to one of them and observe it. It would be impossible to gain the impression that the cicada is wanting to say something to you with the consonantal sound it produces! You have before you the simple fact of an insect in action—that is all! And then, what are we to say of the animals that low or bleat or roar? Such sounds do no more than express defence, resistance or a sense of well-being; they are far from revealing any inner experience of the soul. Finally, in the singing of the birds, you can distinctly feel that the music does not live inside them. The simple and natural feeling about the singing of birds is the same you have when you compare the one or the other variety of it with the corresponding flight, with the beating of the wings. For it is true, there is a harmony between the external movements the bird makes in flight and the music it produces with its voice.

And now, turn right away from the animal world and listen to the inwardness, to the artistic creation of inner experience that reaches you through the vowels as spoken by the human being! Listen again to the experience of the external world to which you have access through the consonants as spoken by the human being. Listen to human speech, listen to it also in its connection with mime and with gesture; and it will not fail to generate in you a true and proper feeling for the significance of the human being in the universe. For it is truly revealed to you in what speech can become in the human being.

Then your heart and soul will be given the correct orientation, and the way will lie open for you to enter further into the more esoteric aspect of our theme. And this is what we shall be doing in the remaining lectures.

'In the current epoch of the earth'

Telegram to Marie Steiner in Berlin

[Dornach, 14 March 1923]

Fondest birthday thoughts. Letter follows.

Rudolf Steiner

To Marie Steiner in Berlin

Dornach, 15 March 1923

I hope that you received the birthday telegram. More fond birthday thoughts follow with this letter. I enclose with these thoughts the content in verse form of my lecture here on Sunday:[7]

> In the current epoch of the earth
> The human being needs renewed
> Spiritual content for the words he speaks;
> For during the period spent in sleep outside the body
> Soul and spirit retain from speech
> Those things which in the word speak of the spirit;
> For human beings in sleep must
> Aspire to commune with the Archangels.
> And they absorb only spirit content
> Not material content of words.
> If a human being lacks this communion
> His whole being suffers.

I am glad to hear that things are going well in Berlin. Your letter arrived only this morning. I started on the eurythmy forms for the poems immediately. I think that they are a success. I will enclose them with this letter. I will keep the originals here and send copies made by Bauer.

Goetheanum stage group, Dornach.

5. How eurythmy arises out of anthroposophy

Rudolf Steiner described his work as 'anthroposophy' as early as 1902. He meant by this that his lectures would open the door to the spiritual world by deepening knowledge of the human being's spiritual nature. The first selection in this section is an introductory lecture prior to a eurythmy performance that tells about the spiritual nature that indwells the physical body. In this context, we learn that speech comes forth from an activity between the spiritual and physical in the human being, from the interplay of the inner world and the outer world.

The next selection is a series of photos and excerpts that give an impression of the natural harmony between the internal architecture of the first Goetheanum and the moving eurythmists who performed on the stage there. Rudolf Steiner created the forms of the building and eurythmy out of the same 'soul state'.

The concluding piece gives a hint how to recognize the living, evolving being of eurythmy as one would a human being or a plant. In the spirit of Goethe's theory of plant metamorphosis, speech is the element that reveals the human being in the same way as the leaf reveals the plant. Eurythmy takes the next turn in metamorphosis and allows world riddles in the highest sense to come to expression. Anthroposophically oriented spiritual science and the artistic development of eurythmy stand on the ground of Goetheanism.

Introductory words to a delegates' congress

Before the eurythmy performance today, I wish to say a few words to illustrate how eurythmy proceeds from that spiritual conception which anthroposophy can give. Numerous anthroposophical friends are with us today, many of whom have come from a far distance. May I therefore be permitted to base my remarks on this occasion on anthroposophical foundations, to say a few purely anthroposophical words about eurythmy.

Whatever proceeds from the human being—be it thoughts or feelings or impulses of will, or speech or song, recitation or declamation—all this proceeds not from any one part of human nature, but in every case from a totality of human nature. To see how the human being reveals himself in any single instance is only possible if we observe the part that is played by the several elements of a person's nature in any such human manifestation. The spiritual knowledge out of which we are speaking is no less exact than any branch of science in the learned life of today—indeed, it is far more precise. Speaking in the light of this knowledge, we must divide the human being as follows. He has his physical body, then the first super-sensory member of his being—the so-called etheric body or body of formative forces—and, then, what is connected already with the inner life of the soul, the astral body. Lastly there is the organization of the ego.

In one aspect, we have the entire human being before us when with the vision of the soul we confront these four elements of the human being. According to their several basic forces and components, these four elements are concerned in every manifestation of the human being. The only question is, what part they play. Naturally, I can only give brief hints in what I now have to say. However, this being a meeting of anthroposophists from all over the world, I should like to speak of eurythmy, for once, quite anthroposophically. Popular explanations can be given on other occasions.

To begin with, let me remind you of this fact: every time a person is in the sleeping state, his ego organization and astral body are separated from the physical body and from the etheric or life-body or body of formative forces. Now the ego and astral body are thereby in a way related to the things and processes of the earth, albeit the human being is not immediately conscious of the fact. In truth, with our real inner being — that is, with our ego and astral body — we are not so intimately related to the outer world in waking life as we are unconsciously during sleep. For in our waking condition we can only perceive the outer world with the aid of the physical body and its organization, and with the aid of the etheric body and its organization. On the other hand, every time we are asleep throughout our earthly life, the ego and astral body become associated intimately with the outer world. Hence the relation of ego and astral body to the outer world is very close and inti-mate, if I may so describe it, and for this very reason they can mediate for all that enters unconsciously into the conscious life in the manifestations of the human being.

Suppose, for example, that we speak. We speak in vowels and in consonants. To the way of thought which is almost exclusively recognized in our time — that of the senses and of the intellect combining the sense impressions — speech is bound to the physical body, it arises from the formation of certain organs. It is quite true, what happens in the physical body when we speak can be described more or less exactly; but the other — supersensory — members of the human being's nature also play a most important part in all our speech.

Let us first think what the etheric body, or body of formative forces, signifies for the human being. This supersensory body is nearest to the physical body, and in the night — in sleep — it does not separate from the physical. The etheric or life-body or 'body of formative forces' is the bearer of the element of thought — the bearer of all those forces in the human being which form his thought. We form our thoughts with the help of the physical and the etheric body and are far removed from thought in sleep (we only just encounter it, in our dreams, in falling asleep and on awakening, and even then only chaotically) because, in sleep, we are separated with the ego and the astral body from that part which contains our thought life.

In truth, we think throughout the night but are simply not aware of it. The thinking lives in the etheric or life-body. And that is also the reason why the education we receive with regard to our physical body as well as our etheric body, or body of formative forces, is more important than we generally perceive for the way in which people think. If a person receives a slapdash education with regard to the handling of his organization, if I can put it like that, then this also comes to expression in the slapdash handling of his thoughts. The way in which a person is inwardly organized, including his body of formative forces, is reflected in his thinking. And what flows into speech or, indeed, singing as thinking comes from the physical body and from the etheric body or body of formative forces. But—concentrating on speech—it is actually the elements of the external world that flow into speech. We must recognize in speech what enters into speech and singing through the ego and astral body via the breathing and blood circulation. What enters into speech and singing via the breathing and blood circulation comes from the ego and astral body, which have the opportunity always to connect intimately with the inner world when they are separated from the external world.

If we want to investigate, for example, the curious shape the lips take to form certain consonants, we cannot stop at the human being if we want to learn about the—I might almost say—mysterious shape of the lips, tongue and so on. In this respect our so-called scientific age today is extraordinarily superficial.

As you know, there are two language theories which are becoming less important but once caused a great stir. They are called the ding-dong theory and the bow-wow theory. Now these matters have been argued by scholars and the contributions in this respect can be read in greater detail in the writings of the Oxford professor Max Müller than I can set them out here. But essentially the ding-dong theory posits that when the bell rings something of the inner nature of the external object resounds and that a person can enter into the processes and objects of the external world not just through the hearing but through the perception of the other senses as well. This process is not quite as external as presented by the ding-dong theory but it arises through the intimate communion which ego and astral body enter into when they are separated from the external world.

Now just as we have memory in ordinary life, so do the astral body and ego resonate in us, so to speak; they continue to have an after-effect. We are not conscious of this after-effect of the astral body and the ego. Yet, strange as it may sound, it is not for nothing that we sleep, for the relation then established with the outer world echoes on in us. The ego and astral body carry into us the intimate inner qualities of outer things.

We do not adapt ourselves to the animal sounds externally, as the bow-wow theory of language would assume. Nevertheless, through our ego and our astral body we do experience the outer things. Nor can we understand the wondrous formation of lips and tongue and palate, etc., down to the various speech organs until we realize this fact: the tongue, lips, palate, etc. are formed not only from within outwards, as ordinary physiology may prove, but from the outer world into the human being. The things of the outer world are actually living in the forms of the organs that underlie our speech.

If it were not so, the human could never have attained the faculty of speech. Speech is not merely a revelation of what the human being experiences within him — that is to say, inside his skin. Speech also contains all that is living in the secrets of the earthly things around us, of which we become aware because our ego and astral body are separated again and again from the physical and the etheric. Speech is the very thing we learn in the outer world around us. Even into the vocal chords, all that the ego and astral body discover by their intimate acquaintance with the outer world in sleep is waving, vibrating, echoing. The advanced languages have by now completely polished away and worn away this wondrous kinship, this intimate union of language with the outer world. We need a knowledge deeper than any that is founded on materialist physiology. With deeper knowledge of this kind, we can perceive a fact, the importance of which should not be underrated. When, for example, we pronounce an *i* [phonetic *i*, English *ee*] or an *e* [phonetic *e*, English *a*] it is not a mere manifestation of human nature; it is something which the entire being of a person experiences in communion with the outer world around him.

We need only consider the forms that are conjured up before the vision of the soul as living imaginations when we perceive the relation of a *t* or of a *u* to the things of the outer world.

Anyone who can feel a *t* knows well what lies inherent in it. Rightly felt and sensed, it is like something that works from the outer world so as to lend us our own existence. Hence, all languages which have the *i* sound in the word 'I' give the human being a sense of existence simply through the language. Languages which do not have the *i* sound in the word 'I' cannot give him this sense of existence.

Again, how does the *u* appear to the soul? The *u* is as though two kinds of supersensory elements in the outer world were coming into touch with one another, and the human being must become aware of their contact.

So there are many different pictures, musical or sculptural, which arise before the soul when we try to enter into the intimate qualities of speech.

Only when we understand these pictures can we penetrate into the wonderful union which exists between our life of soul—our life of mind and feeling—and our speech. Then do we learn to recognize how everyday speech reaches up on the one hand to the thinking life of the human being and on the other hand reaches physically downwards to the circulation of the blood. Needless to say, you cannot crudely feel how it changes when you speak *i* or *u*. Nevertheless, in a delicate way the change is there. One might actually speak of a microscopic change of the pulse (figuratively speaking) when a person thoroughly feels what the soul experiences in the course of a word or a sentence—when the soul vividly enters into the intimacies of the spoken sounds or of the notes of song.

We must look in the blood for these human movements which answer to ordinary speech or song and carry within them the thought, that is, essentially the inartistic content. But when we pass from speech to the imaginations (musical or plastic imaginations, or painted in colour), then we feel it possible to express what lies inherent in speech—with the same inner law and principle as in speech itself—through visible movements in space of the various elements or of the human being as a whole. Thus we obtain real visible speech, revealing directly what in audible language can only be revealed by the manner, by the treatment.

If, as we speak, we are able to colour one sound by another—if we are able to treat it poetically and artistically, correctly embodying in it rhythm, melody and theme—then do we enter gradually into the mysteries of declamation and recitation. Frau Dr Steiner has worked at these things for many years, seeking to get beyond the inartistic tendencies of our time, which only look for prosaic emphasis and pathos. Laying stress on the treatment of all that is poetically and artistically shaped in speech, she has sought to attain the true art of recitation and declamation.

This hidden eurythmy is already there, inherent in the very treatment of language. Every true poet has it. True poets, unfortunately, represent only a small percentage of those who are taken as poets nowadays. Ninety per cent, we might say, of those who write poetry today are not poetic artists.

The moment we enter thus into the manner, the inner quality of the way speech is treated, we feel that it provides far greater possibilities to express the life of the soul than the mere prosaic content of the words. The prosaic meaning of the words only conveys the inartistic part. It is in the how, not in the what, that the artistic life is expressed. By a kind of divination, we must always first redeem the artistic element from that which can alone be communicated through the printed words of the poem. The poet, when he lives and expresses himself in speech, feels the entire human being. Again and again I must recall the beautiful poetic saying: *Spricht die Seele, so spricht, ach, schon die Seele nicht mehr.* (When the soul speaks, alas, the soul already speaks no more!) It is quite true of the kind of speech that mainly emphasizes the prosaic meaning. How different is the speech that lives in the plastic form and colouring which sound can give to sound—which the sound-treatment itself can give! How different, again, is speech that lives in the musical element! When the soul speaks this kind of language, it is the soul, above all, which is trying to say what cannot be said through speech that has grown prosaic and inartistic.

This is the very thing we can derive from speech and song through eurythmy, where the most expressive human elements are brought into movement. Eurythmy is not like dance which moves the legs and feet—undoubtedly, the less expressive human members. Although it also moves the legs and feet, these are not the main movements it brings about, and it has no essential kinship with dance. The forms which the arms and hands—those most expressive members of the human body—are given are the true visible speech corresponding to what I have just indicated. Out of such insight into human nature — I have only hinted at it here — we can discover the laws and principles of expression for every finger, for every movement of the arm, for every subtle change of the human organism in space, just as nature or the spirit of nature found the same when in our childhood, out of unconscious human life, it let us learn speech and song in our childlike way. By a like inner law we now can create visible speech, which plays upon another instrument, if I may call it that, the theme which song or declamation or recitation plays. Truly, we come to a kind of orchestral harmony between the eurythmy on the stage and the chords that are struck on the instruments of music, or the sound that emerges in recitation and declamation through the human voice.

Thus we are able to derive from its very fountainhead an art which humankind hitherto could not discover, for the simple reason that every art must first be created out of the special cultural conditions that the successive ages in the life of humanity provide.

In eurythmy we have a new kind of art, making use of the human being himself as an instrument even more than does the art of mime. For the human being is like a microcosm in relation to the macrocosm — he contains within him all the universal secrets. Here we make use of the human being who bears within him all the secrets of the universe, as microcosm in relation to the macrocosm, and by the way we do this we may hope: eurythmy will become in time what it cannot yet be today—a fully justified younger art beside the older arts, which in themselves are fully justified.

First Goetheanum in Dornach, Switzerland, South View.

The building and eurythmy are one

The development of eurythmy is closely connected with the development of the architecture of the Goetheanum. After this wonderful, double-domed building carved in wood had burned down on New Year's Eve 1922, Rudolf Steiner wrote:

And when this art of eurythmy was performed on the stage of the Goetheanum, one was meant to have the feeling that there was a very natural relationship between the moving eurythmists and the stationary forms of the internal architecture and sculpture. The latter was meant to be pleased, as it were, to receive the former. The building and eurythmy movement were meant to grow into one...

If I make no greater claim than this, that such a unity between building forms and the words or music was only being attempted, what I say will not sound too presumptuous. Because no one is more convinced than I am that our achievements are still very imperfect. But I did make the attempt to create the design in such a way that one can feel how the movement of the words naturally runs along the forms of the capitals and architraves...

And I know, too, that I shaped the forms of the building out of the same soul state from which the pictures for eurythmy come. Thus the harmony of the two was not striven for out of an intellectual intention, but arose out of a similar artistic impulse. Probably eurythmy could not have been found without the work on the building. Prior to the idea of the building, it was only present in its first beginnings.

The students were first taught how to create in the soul the moving speech forms in the hall built in the south wing of the Goetheanum. The interior architecture of this hall in particular was intended to be eurythmy at rest, just as the eurythmy movements in the hall were moving sculptural forms, created from the same spirit as the resting forms themselves.

This is the hall where the smoke was first discovered on 31 December, the result of the fire which grew to destroy the whole Goetheanum. Anyone who loved this building felt the pitiless flames painfully burn through the feelings which had been decanted into the forms at rest and the work which took place within them.

First Goetheanum stage as seen from the auditorium.

The stained glass windows

I now want to indicate how our glass windows will unite outside and inside. Each window will be of one colour, but there will be different shades in different places, expressing the way the interplay between outside and inside must have a spiritual harmony. Within each monochrome window there will be thicker and thinner parts, parts where the physical substance is thicker, more solid, and parts where it is thinner. More light will shine in through the thinner parts and less through the thicker ones, which will thus yield darker shades. The interplay between spirit and matter will be discerned in what the windows express; and the whole of the interior surface will strive to be an organ for the speech of the gods. The larynx makes it possible for human beings to speak, and in the same way we shall discern that the whole shaping in relief of our building's interior is an organ with which the gods can speak to us from all directions of the universe. Everywhere there are speech organs of the gods.

What are we aiming for in seeking to make our walls permeable, in seeking to shape them in such a way that they negate themselves so that we can find a way of passing through them by making them into organs of speech for the gods? Our aim is none other than to show that we are searching for the path to the spirit by breaking through our walls and letting the gods use them as organs of speech. When we look at our windows they will tell us in the light and dark shading of their colours: 'Find thus, O human being, the path to the spirit!'

The Christmas Conference — Imagination, Inspiration, Intuition

My dear friends!

Today our guests from further afield who have already arrived make up the majority of those present at this opening performance of eurythmy. There is no need for me to speak particularly about the nature of eurythmy, for our friends know about this from various writings that have appeared in print. But especially since we are gathering once more for an anthroposophical task, I should like to introduce this performance with a few words.

In the first instance, eurythmy is that art which has originated entirely from the soil of anthroposophy. Of course it has always been the case that every artistic activity that was to bring something new into civilization originated in supersensory human endeavour. Whether you look at architecture, sculpture, painting or the arts of music or poetry, you will always find that the impulses visible in the external course of human evolution are rooted in some way in occult, supersensory ground, ground we may seek in connection with the mysteries. Art can only flow into human evolution if it contains within it forces and impulses of a supersensory kind. But the present-day view of art arises in the main from the entirely materialistic tendency in thinking that has seized hold of Europe and America since the fifteenth century. And though a certain kind of scientific knowledge can flourish in this materialism, anything genuinely artistic cannot. True art can only arise out of spiritual life.

Therefore it is as a matter of course that a special art has arisen out of the spiritual life of the anthroposophical movement. It is necessary to understand that art must be born out of the supersensory realm through the mediation of the human being. Considering the descending scale stretching from the supersensory realm down to externally perceptible phenomena, you find the faculty of Intuition at the top, at the point where—if I may put it like this—the human being merges with the spirit. Inspiration has to do with the capacity of the human being to face the supersensory on his own, hearing it and letting it reveal itself. And when he is able to link what he receives through Inspiration so intensely with his own being that he becomes capable of moulding it, then Imagination comes about.

In speech we have something that makes its appearance in an external picture, though it is an external picture which is extraordinarily similar to Inspiration. We might say that what we bear in our soul when we speak resembles Intuition, and what lies on our tongue, in our palate, comes out between our teeth and settles on our lips when we speak is the sense-perceptible image of Inspiration.

But where is the origin of what we push outwards from our inner soul life in speech? It originates in the mobile shape of our body, or I could say in our bodily structure in movement. Our ability to move our legs as well as our

arms and hands and fingers is what gives us our first
opportunity as little children to sense our relationship
with the outside world. The first experience capable of
entering into the consciousness of our soul is what we
have in the physical movement of arms, hands and legs.
The other movements are more connected with the human
being. But the limbs which we stretch out into the space
around us are what gives us a sense of the world. And
when we stretch out our legs in a stride or a leap, or our
arms to grasp something, or our fingers to feel something,
then whatever we experience in doing this streams back to
us. And as it streams back, it seizes hold of tongue, palate
and larynx and becomes speech. Thus through movement,
a person in his organism is an expression of the complete
human being. When you begin to understand this you
sense that what in speech resembles Inspiration can descend into Imagination. We can call back something that is
a gift to our limbs, to our tongue, our larynx and our
palate and so on, we can recall it and let it stream back,
asking: what kind of feelings, what kind of sensations
stream outwards in our organism in order to create the
sound *A*? We shall always discover that an *A* arises
through something that expresses itself in one way or
another in the air, through a particular movement of our
organs of speech, or an *E* in optical axes crossing over, and
so on. Then we shall be able to take what has streamed out
in this way and become a sound or element of speech, and
send it back into our whole being, into our human being of
limbs, thus receiving in place of what causes speech to

resemble Inspiration something else instead, something that can be seen and shaped and which therefore resembles Imagination.

So actually eurythmy came into existence when what works unconsciously in the human being to transform his capacity for movement into speech is subsequently recalled from speech and returned to the capacity for movement. Thus an element that belongs to Inspiration becomes an element belonging to Imagination.

Therefore an understanding of eurythmy is closely linked with discovering through eurythmy how Intuition, Inspiration and Imagination are related. Of course we can only show this in pictures, but the pictures speak clearly.

Consider, dear friends, a poem alive in your soul. When you have entirely identified yourself inwardly with this poem and have assimilated it to such an extent and so strongly that you no longer need any words but have only feelings and can experience these feelings in your soul, then you are living in Intuition. Then let us assume that you recite or declaim the poem. You endeavour, in the vowel sounds, in the harmonies, in the rhythm, in the movement of the consonants, in tempo, beat and so on, to express in speech through recitation or declamation what lies in those feelings. What you experience when doing this is Inspiration. The element of Inspiration takes what lives purely in the soul where it is localized in the nervous system, and pushes it down into the larynx, palate and so on.

Finally, let it sink down into your limbs, so that in your

own creation of form through movement you express what lies in speech; then, in the poem depicted in eurythmy, you have the third element, Imagination.

In the picture of the descent of world evolution down to the human being, you have that scale which human beings have to re-ascend, from Imagination through Inspiration to Intuition. In the poem transformed into eurythmy you have Imagination, in the recitation and declamation, you have Inspiration as a picture, and in the entirely inward experience of the poem, in which there is no need to open your mouth because your experience is totally inward and you are utterly identified with it and have become one with it, in this you have Intuition.

In a poem transformed into eurythmy, experienced inwardly and recited, you have before you the three stages, albeit in an external image. In eurythmy we are dealing with an element of art which had from inner necessity to emerge out of the anthroposophical movement. What you have to do is bring to consciousness what it means to achieve knowledge of the ascent from Imagination to Inspiration, and to Intuition.

Christmas Conference — eurythmy is a moving sculpture

Introductory words to the eurythmy performance given in Dornach, 26 December 1923, on the occasion of the foundation meeting of the General Anthroposophical Society.

The nature of eurythmy has often been discussed in the presence of many different groups of friends, and only recently a wide-ranging presentation was given at the Goetheanum [see Rudolf Steiner's introduction to a eurythmy performance in *Das Goetheanum,* vol. 3, no. 7, 23 September 1925]. It is certainly not necessary to speak at this performance, which is exclusively for our friends, about the essential nature of eurythmy, about the basic principles, which are familiar to all of you. Yet I should like to characterize once more from a certain standpoint both how eurythmy is positioned in the artistic development of the present and what its position among the arts in general is. Today I will speak a few words about how eurythmy must, in fact, by its very nature be drawn from the essence of the human being by a spiritual world conception that, in accordance with our time, is making itself felt in our present age.

Let us look at another art that portrays the human being—the art of sculpture, which shows him in his quiescent form. Whoever approaches sculpture with a certain feeling for form, whoever experiences the human being, human characteristics, through a sculptural work of art does so in the best way when he feels: here the human being is silent, speaking through his quiescent form. Now we know that in the eighteenth century Lessing wrote a paper on the limits of the plastic arts (it was not called that, but that was its content) in which he said that sculpture should by its very nature be a manifestation of that which is at rest, which is still in the human being — a being placed in the cosmos so sculpture can only express what manifests itself as silence, as stillness in the human being. Hence any attempt to represent the human being in movement through the medium of sculpture will undoubtedly prove to be an artistic error.

In times gone by, indeed up to the time of the Renaissance, it was a matter of course that sculpture could only represent the human being in a state of rest. This period, which began with ancient Greece and ended with the Renaissance, was mainly concerned with the development in the human being of the intellectual soul. With regard to the inner configuration of the human being — sentient soul, mind soul and consciousness soul — it is the mind soul, embracing as it does all that is connected with the human mind, that holds the middle place; and the mind is in fact permeated with that quiescent feeling which also comes to expression in the quiescent human form.

We live today in an age in which we must advance from the feeling element in the human being to the will element; for fundamentally speaking it is the descent into the will element which, if consciously undertaken, would enable us today to achieve spiritual insight.

This brings us to the point where we may turn our spiritual gaze to the human being in movement; not to the human being who, as the expression of the cosmic Word, remains silent in order to rest in form, but to the human being as he stands in the living motion of the cosmic Word, bringing his organism into activity in accordance with his cosmic environment.

It is this element in the human being that must find expression in eurythmy. And if we are able to observe things from the point of view of the spiritual science which is appropriate for the humanity of today, we will always have the feeling that form must become fluid. Let us look at a human hand. Its silence finds expression in its quiescent form. What then is the meaning of this quiescent form when the human being as a whole is taken into consideration? Its meaning is apparent when the quiescent element of feeling is allowed to hold sway as it did from the age of the ancient Greeks to the time of the Renaissance. There is certainly great meaning in such a gesture as this, in which I indicate something with my hand, then allow it to remain in a state of rest. But it does not enable us to understand what must be realized today with regard to the human being; it does not enable us to understand the human being in his totality.

It is indeed impossible to understand the human form when observing the human being as a whole, unless one is conscious of the fact that every motionless form in the human being has meaning only because it is able to pass over into definite movement. What would the significance of the human hand be if it were compelled to remain motionless? Even in its motionless state the form of the hand is such as to demand movement. When we study the human being with that inner mobility that is essential to the spiritual science of today, then from out of the quiescent form movement reveals itself on all sides. It is not too much to say that anyone who visits a museum containing sculpture belonging to the best periods of plastic art, and who looks at the figures with the inner vision arising out of the spiritual knowledge of our time, will see these figures descend from their stands, move about the room and meet each other, becoming on all sides filled with movement. And eurythmy — well, eurythmy arises naturally out of sculpture. It is also our task to learn to understand this. Today people gifted with a certain spiritual mobility feel disturbed if obliged to look for a long time at a motionless Greek statue. They have to force themselves to do it. This can, and indeed must be done in order not to spoil the Greek statue in one's own personal imagination. But at the same time the urge remains to bring movement into this motionless form. As a consequence there arises that moving sculpture to which we give the name of eurythmy. Here the cosmic Word is itself, is movement. In eurythmy the human being is no longer silent but through his movement communicates innumerable cosmic secrets.

It is indeed always the case that the human being communicates through his own being innumerable secrets of the universe. One can, however, have yet another cosmic feeling. Anyone who has a living understanding of such descriptions of cosmic evolution as are to be found in my *Outline of Occult Science* will realize from the outset that, in the case of the human form of today, it is as though one had allowed an inner mobility to become dried up, to become rigid. One need only to look back to the time of the Old Moon. The human being was then in a continual state of metamorphosis. Such a definitely formed nose, such

Eurythmy symphony – Flutes

definitely formed ears as the human being has today did not exist at that time. The once mobile forms had to become frozen. People today often appear as frozen, immobile beings, incapable of metamorphosis, to anyone who with his vision can transport himself into the time of the Old Moon. And what we achieve by means of eurythmy, when we make it into a visible speech, is no less than this. The bringing of movement, of fluidity, into the frozen human form.

This demands a type of study that must in its very nature be artistic. In this sphere everything of an intellectual nature is positively harmful. Eurythmy is and must remain an art.

Just consider for a moment how a eurythmy form as you have sometimes seen here for poems that have the profundity in terms of their experience and structure of the poems of Steffen for example, just consider how such a form would best be found when, let us say, one imagines ten or twelve people of the present day. You are certainly all individually different with regard to your external form; but one can say of every person, no matter whether he has a round or long head, a pointed or blunt nose, how he would move his etheric body with a poem. And it would certainly be interesting to take the people sitting in a given row and show how, in a poem, each of those sitting here would move in accordance with his own form if this arose entirely from the individual characteristics of the person concerned. Here, for instance, eight people are sitting in this row. In such a case quite different eurythmy forms would arise from the human form. This would be very interesting. One would have to look at many people in order to say how the human being would move for *Und es wallet und woget und brauset und zischt.*

And then one gets the idea of how the forms are born of necessity. Thus eurythmy is born wholly out of the moving human form, but one must be able to take up such a standpoint that, when asked why the form for a poem is such and such, one must say: well, that is how it is! If anyone demands an intellectual explanation in justification of such a form, then one will feel annoyed to give it because that is really inartistic. Eurythmy is created entirely out of feeling and can also only be understood through feeling.

Of course one must learn certain things, the letters must be learned, and so on. But after all, when you write a letter, here also you do not think about how an *i* or a *b* is written, but you write because you are able do so. The point, then, is not how the eurythmist learns *a, b, c* but to enjoy what results as the end product.

A newly created moving sculpture must develop out of eurythmy. And for this living sculpture one will of course make use of the human being himself; here we cannot use clay or marble. This leads into a realm of art which, in the profoundest sense, touches reality just where sculpture departs from it. Sculpture portrays what is dead in the human being, or at least what is deathlike in its rigidity. Eurythmy portrays everything in the human being which is of the nature of life itself. For this reason eurythmy can

Eurythmy symphony – Orchestra

give us a feeling of how the universal cosmic life laid hold of the human being and placed him into earthly evolution, giving him his earthly task. There is perhaps no other art through which we can experience the human being's relationship to the cosmos so vividly as we are able to do through the art of eurythmy. Therefore this art of eurythmy, based as it is on the etheric forces in the human being, had to appear just at the time that a modern spiritual science was being sought. For it was out of this modern spiritual science that eurythmy had to be born.

Eurythmy programme for members

Dornach, 20. April 1924, 11 Uhr (Ostern)
Dornach, 22. April 1924, 17 Uhr

EURYTHMY-PROGRAMM
für Mitglieder

I

Die Grundsteinlegung . . . . Rudolf Steiner
Air aus der Suite, D-Dur (bearb. f. Cello und Klavier)
. . . . J. S. Bach
Aus «Wegzehrung» . . . . Albert Steffen
    Du hebst die Hände ...
    Für meine Mutter
Präludium, f-moll . . . . J. S. Bach
Aus «Wegzehrung»: Christus in mir . . . . Albert Steffen
Andante . . . . J. E. Galliard

II

Menuett für Flöte und Klavier . . . . Rosenberg
Aus «Wegzehrung» . . . . Albert Steffen
   Wie die Blumen im Garten stehn, . . .
   Liegt der bloße Erdenleib . . .
Largo, B-Dur, für Violine und Oboe . . . . G. Fr. Handel
Vermächtnis . . . . Robert Hamerling
Präludium. . . . . Pugnani-Kreisler

The Foundation Stone

Today's eurythmy performance is presented in the spirit
that the important events in the anthroposophical movement since the Christmas Conference at the Goetheanum
should receive a new character. The aim was to give an
impulse that was not just temporary but would be sustained and develop. The only way we will make progress
in the anthroposophical movement is not to keep making
a new start, as we have done so far, but to make sure that
those things which have been initiated really are properly
carried forward.

   That is why you will see here today what was presented
for the first time at the Christmas Conference. You will hear
the words whose purpose was to be laid in our hearts at the
Christmas Conference as the Foundation Stone for the newly
created Anthroposophical Society. Today you will see these
words transformed into eurythmy, and in this way what was
started at Christmas will be carried one step forward.

This performance will be followed by the presentation in eurythmy of poetic works that are exceptionally appropriate for the Easter festival. In this way, this performance is intended as a continuation of the things we attempted to give at Christmas as a new beginning. And it is to be hoped that as an awareness of the significance, the long-term significance, of the Christmas conference increasingly enters the hearts of our dear friends of the Anthroposophical Society we will be able to continue along this path. Then the anthroposophical movement will be more than a kind of pearl necklace in which the pearls are lined up next to one another; it will be something which grows, sprouts, buds and continues to develop in its growing, sprouting and budding.

About the Being of eurythmy

The art of eurythmy is, without doubt, only just at the beginning of its work. We might even go as far as to describe it as the intention to give something a try. As a result, you will permit me to say a few words about the being of the art of eurythmy.

Everything that is being tried and that will in future be perfected with regard to the art of eurythmy is based on the Goethean perception of the world and life. The Goethean perception of the world and life results in a particularly artistic approach and a specific view of art. And that, precisely, is the special thing about Goethe, that he was able in his own philosophy to build a bridge, a quite natural bridge, between artistic attitude, artistic force and general world conception. Thus on the basis of a Goetheanistic approach, on which our anthroposophical science of the spirit is based, we could attempt to create something in a very special field, in the field of the art of human movement, which is wholly the expression of a Goethean artistic attitude.

That is also why I ask you not to think that we are trying in some way to compete with what we are able to present in this respect at the present time already with any art or art form that might be seen as related in some way to the art of eurythmy. We have no intention of doing that. We know very well that the art of dance and similar arts which might be mistaken for ours have reached such a level of perfection today that we cannot hope to compete with them in any way. And, indeed, that is not what we aim to do; we are concerned to introduce something fundamentally new into the general development of the arts in human development. And without resorting to theory, I would like to set out very briefly how our endeavours are connected with the greatness of the Goethean perception of the world.

The actual significance, the great and incisive aspects of the Goethean perception of the world have by no means been sufficiently recognized. Goethe was able to give direction to his world of ideas, his world of cognitive perception, in such a way that he was truly able to ascend from a science of the lifeless—which basically still comprises all our science today—to a certain cognition of life.

It only gives the appearance of being theoretical when everything points to Goethe's grand idea of the metamorphosis of organic entities and single organic entities. We only need to imagine, as Goethe would have done, how an individual plant develops as a living entity, how it grows, reaches perfection and the peak of its development. *For Goethe, each individual leaf*—be it the green plant leaves or colourful petals—*basically represents the whole plant*, only on a simpler level than the whole plant, and the whole plant is, in turn, only a complicated leaf for him.

Goethe applied this immensely important perception to all living beings. Each living entity is developed such that as a whole it is the complex development of each of its components and each component in turn reveals the living entity, only on a simpler level. Now this view can be transferred to the forms of expression and activities of any living being, and in particular the highest living being that the human being knows within his world: the human being himself. And thus we can say, following Goethe, that human language, too, is an individual aspect of human nature. *What the human being expresses through speech from the depths of his soul using his larynx and associated organs represents the expression of a single organ, a revelation of the human being.* Anyone who is able to see the potential forces, the realms of activity and movement potentials in the human larynx during speech, particularly during artistic speech, the speaking of poetry or singing; anyone who can see that and is not so limited as to ignore what the larynx achieves in terms of movement and merely hears the sound produced by the movement; anyone who can do that will be able to transfer to the whole human being what is otherwise expressed only in the single organ — the larynx and its associated organs — during speech.

It is possible to turn the whole of the human being into a larynx so that he moves his limbs in the same way that the larynx is disposed to move in speech or singing. We might also say that when we speak we are dealing with the wave movements of the air. Sound is movements in the air. We do not, of course, see those movements in the air in ordinary life. But anyone who can see them has gained the possibility of transferring those movements to the whole human being, to his limbs. Visible speech is created when a person moves his arms and other limbs in this way in accordance with specific laws. And when the poetic and artistic element in language, the element of song, the musical element is revealed in such visible speech, a wholly new art form arises. That is what eurythmy is intended to be.

To begin with, what you see presented here is nothing more than the artistic expression of the movements of the human larynx transferred to the whole human being. Of course, what is intended to be art and must make a direct aesthetic impression as we watch it if it is to be artistic in its direct effect must have its source in the depths of human nature. In this sense we can say that we must bring to expression in the human being those elements which are disposed in him simply because it is a human organism. Thus there is nothing artificial or contrived in eurythmy. All gestures, all mime, are avoided. Just as in music it is not a matter of expressing something through any given single tone, but of following the principles contained in the progression of tones, so in eurythmy it is not a matter of the hand or any other limb making an arbitrary gesture but of the sequence of movements of the human limbs according with the laws of eurythmy. In this way anything of an arbitrary nature is avoided, and where something arbitrary does occur, you are quite entitled to consider it to be an imperfection. If two people or two groups of people were to present the same item, their depiction would be different only to the extent that the presentation of a Beethoven symphony by two different pianists would be different.

Everything in eurythmy is a copy of the movements of the larynx and its associated organs. But human language is infused with soul warmth, enthusiasm, joy, pain and suffering, and inner crises. All those things which infuse human language as inner expressions of soul are expressed in the reciprocal relationship between the forms, the groups and what the person can reveal in space through his movements. Thus the inner mood of soul brings to expression what infuses the sound from the depths of the soul. Thus you will see on the one hand what is a visible voice. It will be accompanied either by music, which is no more than the other, the parallel expression of the same thing, or mainly by recitation of poetic works. Here it should be noted that in having eurythmy accompanied by poetic works we must take into account that what we have today as recitation and declamation is very much in decline. If we want to have eurythmy accompanied by poetic works, we must return to older, good forms of recitation, of the art of recitation. It is not a matter of bringing the normal prose content of the poetic work to expression by particular emphases, but quite apart from the pure prose content it is the actual artistic part that should be brought to expression through recitation — rhythm, rhyme, the pulsation of the artistic in a poetic work, everything that lies outside the content, in other words, the poetic and musical element. There is little understanding of this in the present time.

But we need only recall that Goethe conducted his *Iphigenie* with a baton or that Schiller had a general melody in his soul before he brought the prose content of a poem to life in his poetic works, that is, he started from the general artistic element. The emphasis on the content nowadays when reciting is nonsense and illustrates the decline. We could not accompany eurythmy with such an art of recitation which only looks at the content. That is why we must return to something that is little understood as recitation by our contemporaries. Thus we believe that through eurythmy we can lend emphasis to the artistic element in the present day and to bring to life something of the Goethean attitude to art. As Goethe so nicely said, those to whom nature begins to reveal its open secret will feel an irresistible longing for its worthiest extension — art. He sees in art the revelation of secret laws of nature which would not be revealed in the absence of art.

That becomes particularly apparent when we see how

the human being in his movements expresses visible, living speech. Goethe said in another place: art consists of a type of cognition in that we grasp the essence of things in tangible and visible forms. And the climax of external nature, the human being, is revealed to us if we can make visible what is contained in his movements and place it before our eyes. That is why we feel very much in tune with Goethe when he says: placed at the summit of nature, the human being in turn sees himself as nature in its completion, which again has to produce a climax. He rises to this task in that he permeates himself with all perfections and virtues, calls on choice, order, harmony and meaning, and finally rises to the production of a work of art.

We believe that the art of eurythmy, which is produced out of the human being himself, at the same time makes something visible to the human eye that is like an artistic revelation of the cosmic mystery that reaches its highest expression in the human being. So far, however, all these things are only present in their beginnings. We know that very well and are our own severest critics of the imperfections that still adhere to our artistic attempts at eurythmy. I would ask you to take today's performance in this spirit. If this begins to be understood among our contemporaries, then it will lead to its further perfection. Because as much as we are convinced that it is still in its infancy today, we are convinced to the same extent that it contains the principles that will enable it to be brought to such perfection by ourselves or by others that the art of eurythmy will be able to present itself as fully legitimate alongside other arts.

Notes

Part One (pages 11–135)

1. Rudolf Steiner's expositions on the path towards human spiritual development were originally published as single essays under the title *Knowledge of the Higher Worlds and its Attainment.* GA 10.

2. Founded in 1875 out of the drive to integrate ancient religion and evolutionary science. The first president, Henry Olcott, worked with Madame Helena Blavatsky, who was a prime force in the development of theosophical doctrine. The second president was Annie Besant. Rudolf Steiner was General Secretary of the German Section of the Theosophical Society from 1902 to 1913.

3. Marie von Sivers, 1867–1948. Rudolf Steiner's collaborator and wife. Her work with him developed the arts of creative speech, drama and the new art of eurythmy. She was central in the task of seeing that Rudolf Steiner's lectures were transcribed, written and published.

4. From *Autobiography*, by Rudolf Steiner, Anthroposophic Press, Hudson, NY, 1999, GA 28. See Steiner's lectures at Dornach, September 1921, in *Speech and Drama.*

5. From *Autobiography*. In connection with the Theosophical Congress in Munich, May and June 1907, when Edouard Schuré's *Sacred Drama of Eleusis* was performed, Steiner gave the lecture cycle *The Theosophy of the Rosicrucian*, London 1981. In August 1910 when Steiner's first mystery drama, *The Portal of Initiation*, was first presented in Munich, he gave a

lecture cycle *The Biblical Secrets of Creation*, London 1944. On 17 August, Steiner's second mystery drama, *The Soul's Probation*, was first performed, followed by ten lectures, *Wonders of the World, Ordeals of the Soul, and Revelations of the Spirit*, London 1983. On 24 August his third mystery drama, *The Guardian of the Threshold*, was performed for the first time followed by a cycle of lectures *On Initiation, Eternity and the Passing Moment; On Spirit Light and the Darkness of Life*, Spring Valley, NY, 1980. In August 1913, Steiner's fourth mystery drama was performed in Munich, *The Soul's Awakening*. This occasion marked the first public performance of eurythmy, an anthroposophic movement art. Steiner also delivered a series of lectures on how to understand his mystery plays, *The Secrets of the Threshold*, London and Hudson, NY, 1987. See Henry Barnes, *A Life for the Spirit*, Hudson, NY, 1998, chapter 5, 'The Work Unfolds'.

6. From *Autobiography*. See references in notes 215 and 395.

   Note 215: See Steiner's lecture in Berlin, 28 October 1909, 'The Spiritual Being of Art', *in Art as Spiritual Activity: Rudolf Steiner's Contribution to the Visual Arts*, Michael Howard, ed., Hudson, NY, 1998; the lectures of 29–30 December 1914, in *Art in the Light of Mystery Wisdom*, London 1998; also the lectures published in *The Arts and their Mission*, New York 1964. In a lecture in Berlin, 4 February 1913, Steiner recalled a 'deep impression that should not be forgotten, an impression of an art exhibition in Vienna when, in 1888, [I] saw for the first time some paintings by Boecklin: his *Pietà*, his *Play of the Waves*, the *Spring Magic*, and the *Nymph of the Fountain*. These paintings induced [me] to occupy [myself] incessantly with the art of painting' (*The Anthroposophic News Sheet*, Dornach, vol. 14, 1946).

Note 395: see Steiner's lecture in the lecture cycle *Colour*, London 1997; also *Art as Seen in the Light of Mystery Wisdom*, London 1996. Also see *Art as Spiritual Activity: Rudolf Steiner's Contribution to the Visual Arts*, introduced and edited by Michael Howard, Hudson, NY, 1998.

7. In *Cosmosophy*, vol. II, GA 208, Rudolf Steiner refers specifically to the forces that become alive after death. He describes on pages 30 and 31 of the 1997 edition, Completion Press, Glympie, Australia, that when we come to earth at birth we receive our physical and ether bodies. When we have gone through the gate of death, we receive as garments our Life Spirit and Spirit Man (Buddhi and Atma in other sources), in summary, the principles that make up the human being.

During life on earth	During life between death and rebirth
I	
Astral body	Spirit human being (atma)
Ether body	Life spirit (buddhi)
Physical body	Spirit self (manas)
	I

8. See selection 2, from *Wisdom of Man*, for a discussion of the second sense, the sense of our own movements from the point of view of the astral body. Yet another point of view, that of the ego organization in relation to human movement, may be found in *Fundamentals of Therapy*, Rudolf Steiner Press, London 1967, pp. 24–9. In the chapter titled 'Why Man is Subject to Illness', Drs Steiner and Wegman contrast sleep with pain and then observe the transition from the painful movement of a limb to its paralysis. 'In the movement accompanied by pain we have the initial stages of a movement paralysed.' In health, the ego-organization is loosely

united with the limb. It unites with the limb in the act of movement and withdraws again at once. As the ego withdraws, the limb follows as outer physical movement. In paralysis, the ego organization dives down into the limb permanently and is no longer able to withdraw.

9. Initiation is a stage of the inner development of the soul and spirit of a human being resulting from undertaking certain esoteric exercises as described by Rudolf Steiner in *Knowledge of the Higher Worlds and Its Attainment*.

10. See chapter 4 of Rudolf Steiner's *An Outline of Esoteric Science*, GA 13, for a detailed historical discussion of this time period. It encompasses about a 12,000 year period beginning with the Atlantean flood (known from the Old Testament story of Noah and the Ark), from which the very ancient East Indian culture arose. The epoch will end with what is called in spiritual science the War of All Against All. The fifth post-Atlantean culture age (about 1500 to the present) within the fifth epoch is characterized by the soul's loss of direct perception of the supersensory world, and attention is directed more to the world of the senses and its control.

11. Plato, 431–351 BC. Descendant of the ancient kings of Athens. Founded the Academy, near Athens, considered the first European university. He believed in the importance of scientific training for wise political action.

12. Anastasius Grün, 1806–76. Born Anton Alexander von Auersperg. Poet.

13. *Der Wolkendurchleuchter,* the first poem ever done in eurythmy. Written by Rudolf Steiner for the first eurythmists. Translation by Juliet Compton-Burnett: 'He who illuminates the clouds, May he illuminate, May he irradiate, May he inspire And fill with warmth and light, Even me.'

Eurythmy as Visible Speech, GA 279, Anthroposophical Publishing Company, London 1955. See the articles 'About the Mantra the Cloud Illuminator' by Ernst Katz and 'Eurythmy Verse' by Rudolf Steiner for translations of this verse into English and other languages in the *Eurythmy Association Newsletter*, XLVIII, Summer 2000.

14. Rudolf Steiner gave a lecture in Arnhem, 18 July 1924 *(Karmic Relationships*, vol. VI, GA 240, Rudolf Steiner Press, London 1971, pp. 120-1) in which he stated, '...[the Anthroposophical Movement] represented as it were the earthly projection of something that exists in the spiritual worlds in a certain stream of the spiritual life. What was taught here on the earth and communicated as anthroposophical wisdom — this was the reflection of the stream flowing in spiritual worlds through the present phase of the evolution of mankind.'

15. From *Karmic Relationships*, vol. VI: 'The Anthroposophical Society was then a kind of "administrative organ" for the anthroposophical knowledge flowing through the Anthroposophical Movement... Since the Christmas Foundation Meeting in Dornach, the opposite of what went before must be recognized: no distinction is to be made henceforward between Anthroposophical Movement and Anthroposophical Society, for they are now identical.'

16. Henri Felix Smits-Mess'oud Bey, died end of November 1911 of heart failure, age 48. He was the husband of Clara and father of Lory.

17. Lory Smits. Born Eleonore Clara Maria Smits-Mess'oud Bey, 1893-1971. She was the first eurythmist.

18. Building in Dornach, Switzerland named for Johann Wolfgang v. Goethe, designed by and dedicated to Rudolf

Steiner's anthroposophical spiritual science. It is the world centre for the Anthroposophical Society, and an auditorium for lectures and artistic performances throughout the year.

19. 507 BC to c. 350 BC.

20. Franz Brentano, 1838–1917. Psychologist and philosopher. One of the pioneers of phenomenology.

21. Herbert Spencer, 1820–1903. English philosopher who interpreted his world-view on the principle of evolutionary progress. Author of *Synthetic Philosophy*.

22. John Stuart Mill, 1806–73. British philosopher and economist.

23. A unit or foot in a line of poetry consisting of one weak and one strong or one short and one long syllable.

24. A unit or foot in a line of poetry consisting of one strong and one weak or one long and one short syllable. In different languages, the stress and length of syllable may or may not be combined.

25. Quote from Friedrich Schiller.

26. Linguistic theory that words developed as a correspondence between sound and meaning.

27. Linguistic theory that language is an imitation of natural sources.

28. Johann Wolfgang von Goethe, 1749–1832. Born in Frankfurt. German poet, dramatist, novelist and scientist. Author of the great dramatic poem *Faust*.

29. Friedrich von Schiller, 1759–1805. Dramatist, poet, historian. One of the founders of modern German literature. He studied medicine, became an army surgeon, but soon turned to writing, winning public acclaim for *Die Raüber* in 1781. He was later a professor of history at the University of Jena, and became a very close friend of Goethe.

30. St Ambrose, 340–97. Bishop of Milan. Inspired the conver-

sion of St Augustine. Wrote hymns, the style of which is still in use.

31. St Augustine, 354–430. Bishop of Hippo. Student of St Ambrose. Son of St Monica. Wrote *Confessions*, *City of God*, *On the Trinity*, *Against Faustus*.

32. *Theosophy: an introduction to the supersensory knowledge of the world and the destination of man*, Rudolf Steiner's book describing the human being as a citizen of three worlds, body, soul and spirit. GA 9, Anthroposophic Press, 1971.

33. Human beings living at the historic time of Atlantis, mentioned in Plato's *Timaeus* and described in detail in Rudolf Steiner's *An Outline of Esoteric Science* and *Cosmic Memory*.

34. The interval forms have become essential elements in the practice of tone eurythmy. This lecture, which is the only source for these forms, was given for Waldorf teachers and a few specially invited eurythmists and eurythmy students. Each form is a quality, a 'rhythm', carried, as Steiner describes in the lecture, on the waves of the blood circulation from the heart to the limbs, and is arrested in the limbs as will. The forms are drawn in the book as they would appear to the onlooker, that is, with the audience seated at the front of the stage, the bottom of the page. Rudolf Steiner's original drawings were made in chalk and later erased. The first two semicircles shown in the lecture are only indicating backward movements and forward movements and are not the interval forms themselves. Dorothea Mier, artistic director of Eurythmy Spring Valley, NY, in speaking of the early eurythmists' work with Rudolf Steiner, says of these forms, 'the eurythmists who worked with him remember the form of the fourth being a tension filled curve, like an over-full glass of water. Please note the slight curve of the fourth

shown in the sketch here. The seventh form is customarily performed as a curve, without the point, enhancing the awareness of the octave. The essence of these forms is so strong, however, there is no need for pedantry, allowing in fact an amazing scope for individual interpretation.'

35. Anton Bruckner, 1824–96. Austrian organist and composer.

Part Two (pages 136–201)

1. Friedrich Froebel, 1782–1852. The father of the kindergarten system. Educated children through design. Caused major changes in the worlds of early childhood education, art and architecture. Influenced by Johann Pestalozzi and Christian Weiss.

2. Edith Maryon, 1872–1924. English artist, sculptress. One of Rudolf Steiner's closest esoteric pupils and collaborators. Worked together with Rudolf Steiner on the design of the first Goetheanum, the statue of the Representative of Man, and the eurythmy figures.

3. The context indicates Rudolf Steiner is referring here to the major common chord. In the key of C major, this would sound as the tones C, E, G.

4. Rudolf Steiner commonly refers to the ancient Pentathlon: discus throw, javelin, long jump, the stadium-length race and wrestling. The Pentathlon was incorporated into the ancient Olympic Games in 708 BC.

5. Fritz Graf von Bothmer, gymnastics teacher in the first Waldorf School in Stuttgart, Germany. He worked from 1922 to 1938 with Rudolf Steiner's indications for gymnastics in the Waldorf curriculum to develop what is now known as Bothmer Gymnastics®, which has been an essential element in the foundation for Spacial Dynamics®.

6. Workshop at the Goetheanum in Dornach, Switzerland where Rudolf Steiner worked on models for the first and second Goetheanum buildings.
   See also footnote on p. 157.

7. The moment chemical materials develop out of other substances, where they are particularly reactive.

8. Paul Broca, 1824–80. French pathologist, anthropologist and pioneer in neurosurgery. He localized the brain centre for articulate speech in the third convolution of the left frontal lobe of the brain.

9. Spiritual hierarchies, invisible beings who exist above the earthly human being.

10. See Rudolf Steiner, *Eurythmy as Visible Speech*, GA 279, lecture 4, Anthroposophic Press, New York 1931.

11. From Greek religion and mythology. Gaia is the earth, daughter of Chaos, mother and nourisher of all things. She is the wife of Uranos (the sky) and Pontus (the sea).

12. The very first of the Greek gods, the father to them all. Uranos was a sky-god, son and husband of Gaia.

13. Johann Wolfgang von Goethe, 1749–1832. Born in Frankfurt. German poet, dramatist, novelist and scientist. Author of the great dramatic poem *Faust*.

Part Three (pages 202–227)

1. This introduction to a eurythmy performance was given in the context of three lectures Rudolf Steiner gave in Dornach titled *Moral Impulses and their Physical Manifestations: Taking Up a Spiritual Path*. These have been published in English under the title *Earthly Knowledge and Heavenly Wisdom*, Anthroposophic Press, Hudson, NY, 1991. GA 221.

2. Johann Faust (1480–1538) was a German magician, alchemist

and astrologer. *Faust* is the title of a tragedy by Johann Wolfgang v. Goethe (Part 1 written in 1808, Part 2 completed in 1832). It is also the title of an opera by Charles Gounod, written in 1859. Rudolf Steiner commonly refers to Goethe's play.

3. Philippus Aureolus Paracelsus (born Theophrastus Bombastus von Hohenheim) lived *c.* 1493–1541. He was a Swiss physician and alchemist. Paracelsus advocated the use of specific remedies for specific diseases. Wrote 'On Diseases of Miners'.

4. Christmas Foundation Meeting of the Anthroposophical Society, held in Dornach, Switzerland, December 1923.

5. Native of Stageirus, a small Greek settlement in Thrace, 384–322 BC. Greek philosopher. His father, Nichomachus, was a noted physician. Aristotle studied under Plato, and tutored Alexander the Great from 342 to 339 BC.

6. Alexander III, 356–323 BC. King of Macedonia, conqueror of much of Asia.

7. Parisian, born Alphonse Louis Constant (1810–75). Synthesized secret traditions into what we know today as 'occultism'. Friends with revolutionary socialists. Met Bulwer Lytton. Wrote *Dogme et rituel de la haute magie* in 1855, which was translated into English as *Transcendental Magic: Its Doctrine and Ritual*.

8. Solomon's seal. A mystic symbol of two interlaced triangles, creating a six-pointed star. It is symbolic of the union of soul and body. King Solomon (848–796 BC) reigned over Israel for 40 years before his death at age 52. Famous for his wisdom as a judge and construction of temple.

9. *Philosophy of Freedom — A Philosophy of Spiritual Activity* (GA 4). Rudolf Steiner's book written in 1894 addressing the two

questions: What is the essential nature of the human being? and How do we find the path to freedom, to free spiritual activity?

Part Four (pages 228–250)

1. A unit or foot in a line of poetry consisting of one weak and one strong or one short and one long syllable.

2. Rudolf Steiner's 52 weekly verses written as cosmic lyric meditations.

3. In this context, members of the General Anthroposophical Society.

4. Rudolf Steiner typically wrote on his forms the name of the eurythmist for whom a form was drawn.

5. Rudolf Steiner intended that the School would consist of members in three classes. Only the First Class lessons were completed before Steiner's death. Members of the Anthroposophical Society may participate in the School of Spiritual Science after satisfying a specific application and admission procedure.

6. The text of a faculty meeting with Rudolf Steiner and eurythmy teachers concerning the curriculum goals for a thorough eurythmy training may be found in *Eurythmy: Its Birth and Development*, Rudolf Steiner, Lory Maier-Smits, Marie Steiner, Anastasi Ltd., Weobley, Herefordshire, 2002.

7. Rudolf Steiner is referring to the lecture he gave 11 March 1923 in Dornach, Switzerland. The series is published in English as *The Driving Force of Spiritual Powers in World History* (GA 222, *Die Impulsierung des weltgeschichtlichen Geschehens durch geistige Mächte*). Speaking about the evolution of the ego and astral body, he says in this first lecture, 'after the fourteenth year, after the onset of puberty, it begins to be

necessary for the soul during sleep to bring the echoes of speech into relation with Beings of the spiritual world ... to establish relations with the Archangeloi ...'

Part Five (pages 251–286)

1. Linguistic theory that words developed as a correspondence between sound and meaning.
2. Linguistic theory that language is an imitation of natural sources.
3. Max Müller, 1823–1900. German Sanskrit scholar. Translated the Rig-Veda and the Upanishads.
4. Quote from Friedrich Schiller.
5. Gotthold Ephriam Lessing, 1729–81. German author, poet, dramatist.
6. European historical period beginning in fourteenth-century Italy and continuing for three hundred years. It is marked by a broadening of artistic and literary activity and the beginnings of modern science.
7. Third of four incarnations in the evolution of the Earth, according to Rudolf Steiner's *An Outline of Esoteric Science*, chapter 4.
8. Albert Steffen, 1884–1963. Swiss playwright, novelist, essayist and philosopher. Leader of the Anthroposophical Society executive after Rudolf Steiner's death.
9. Apparently Rudolf Steiner is referring to a line from Friedrich Schiller's poem *The Diver*, written in 1797. From an anonymous translation of 1902: 'And it boils and it roars, and it hisses and seethes.' From a German text for *Der Taucher*: *Und es wallet und seidet und brauset und zischt.*

Sources

1. 'Must I remain unable to speak?' from Rudolf Steiner's *Autobiography*, Anthroposophic Press, 1999. GA 28. The original German text is *Mein Lebensgang*, which appeared first in the weekly news-sheet *Das Goetheanum*, Dornach, 9 December 1923 through 5 April 1925.
2. 'The Supersensible Origin of the Arts' lecture was given 12 September 1920 in Dornach and is published in Rudolf Steiner, *Art as Spiritual Activity*, Anthroposophic Press, 1998. The original German is titled *Kunst und Kunsterkenntnis*. GA 271.
3. 'Impulses of Transformation for Man's Artistic Evolution' is in Rudolf Steiner, *Art as Seen in the Light of Mystery Wisdom*, Rudolf Steiner Press, 1984. GA 275.
4. The selection about Buddhi is from Rudolf Steiner, *Wisdom of Man, of the Soul, and of the Spirit*, Anthroposophic Press, New York 1971. GA 115. It is an excerpt from a lecture given 25 October 1909, titled, 'Supersensible Processes in the Activities of the Human Senses'. The German is a series of twelve lectures titled *Anthroposophie, Psychosophie, Pneumatosophie.*
5. 'About the essence of the gesture' is an introduction to a performance given in Dornach, 15 July 1923. It is published here for the first time in English. The original is titled *Ueber das Wesen der Gebaerde* and is published in Rudolf Steiner, *Eurythmie, die Offenbarung der sprechenden Seele*, Rudolf Steiner Verlag, Dornach 1972. GA 277.
6. *Movement: The Speech of the Soul*, is an introduction to a per-

formance given in Dornach on 27 April 1924 published by Anthroposophical Publishing Company, London, Anthroposophic Press, New York 1928. The German is titled *Die Bewegung als Sprache der Seele* and is found in Rudolf Steiner, *Eurythmie, die Offenbarung der sprechenden Seele*, Rudolf Steiner Verlag, Dornach 1972. GA 277.

7. 'The Cloud Illuminator' is a facsimile of Rudolf Steiner's handwritten poem. It is published in Tatiana Kisseleff, *Eurythmie Arbeit mit Rudolf Steiner*, Verlag die Pforte, Basel 1982. Quote of Lory Maier-Smits from *How the New Art of Eurythmy Began*, Temple Lodge, London 1997.

8. *A Lecture on Eurythmy* is published in Rudolf Steiner, *Eurythmie als sichtbare Sprache*, GA 279, Rudolf Steiner Verlag, Dornach 1979. It was published as an individual lecture by Rudolf Steiner Press, London 1977.

9. *The Essentials of Education* lecture was delivered 10 April 1924 during the educational conference at the Waldorf School in Stuttgart, Germany. It is published in English by Rudolf Steiner Press, London 1982. The German title is *Die Methodik des Lehrens und die Lebensbedingungen des Erziehens*. GA 308.

10. *The Inner Nature of Music* lecture by Rudolf Steiner was given 8 March 1923 in Stuttgart, Germany. It was published in English by Anthroposophic Press, 1983. The German is titled *Das Wesen des Musikalischen und das Tonerlebnis im Menschen*. GA 283.

11. *Eurythmy as Visible Speech*, Rudolf Steiner, Anthroposophical Publishing Company, 1956. *Eurythmie als sichtbare Sprache*, Rudolf Steiner Verlag, Dornach 1979. GA 279.

12. 'Education Towards Inner Freedom', from Rudolf Steiner, *A Modern Art of Education*, Rudolf Steiner Press, 1972. This lecture was delivered 17 August 1923. The German title for

the course is *Gegenwärtiges Geistesleben und Erziehung*. GA 307.

13. The lecture on gymnastics and eurythmy was given Thursday, 1 March 1923, 6:30–8:00 p.m. It is published in *Faculty Meetings with Rudolf Steiner*, vol. 2, Anthroposophic Press, 1998. The German title is *Konferenzen mit den Lehrern der Freien Waldorfschule in Stuttgart*. GA 300b.

14. *Discussions with Teachers*, Rudolf Steiner Press, London 1983. The excerpt is from a discussion Rudolf Steiner had with Waldorf School teachers in Stuttgart on 29 August 1919. The German title is *Erziehungskunst. Seminarbesprechungen und Lehrplanvorträge*. GA 295.

15. Photo of children from the Waldorf School of Saratoga Springs performing *Ethaun*, a Celtic Wonder Tale.

16. 'Boys and Girls at the Waldorf School', lecture given 24[?]August 1922, from Rudolf Steiner, *The Spiritual Ground of Education*, GA 305, Spiritual Science Library, 1989. The German edition is GA 305, titled *Die geistig-seelischen Grundkräfte der Erziehungskunst*.

17. 'Light Course' is from Rudolf Steiner, *First Scientific Lecture Course – Light Course*, Steiner Schools Fellowship, 1977. Titled in German *Geisteswissenschaftliche Impulse zur Entwickelung der Physik*. GA 320.

18. The eurythmy figure sketch is from Rudolf Steiner, *Entwürfe zu den Eurythmiefiguren*, Rudolf Steiner Verlag, Dornach 1984. GA 26.

19. *Wonders of the World, Ordeals of the Soul, and Revelations of the Spirit*, Rudolf Steiner Press, 1983, is a lecture course given by Rudolf Steiner in relation to the second mystery drama, *The Soul's Probation*, August 1911. The German title is *Weltenwunder, Seelenprüfungen und Geistesoffenbarungen*. GA 129.

20. *The Genius of Language*, lecture course by Rudolf Steiner, 2 January 1920, Anthroposophic Press, 1995. The German title is *Geisteswissenschaftliche Sprachbetrachtungen*. GA 299.

21. 'Picture writing, writing, eurythmy' is an introduction to the eurythmy performance in Dornach, 30 October 1920 and is published here for the first time in English. The original German is titled *Bilderschrift – Schrift – Eurythmie* and is published in Rudolf Steiner, *Eurythmie, die Offenbarung der sprechenden Seele*, Rudolf Steiner Verlag, Dornach 1972. GA 277.

22. The programme for a children's performance is published in German in Rudolf Steiner, *Eurythmie, die Offenbarung der Sprechenden Seele*, Rudolf Steiner Verlag, Dornach 1972. GA 277.

23. 'Supersensible Physiology in Education' is a lecture given to Waldorf teachers in Stuttgart, 21 September 1920. It is in Rudolf Steiner, *Balance in Teaching*, Mercury Press, 1983 and in German *Erziehung und Unterricht aus Menschenerkenntnis*. GA 302a.

24. *Fundamentals of Therapy* is a book co-authored by Rudolf Steiner, Ph.D. and Ita Wegman, M.D., Rudolf Steiner Press, 1967. It was published in German in 1925 with the title *Grundlegendes für eine Erweiterung der Heilkunst nach geisteswissenschaftlichen Erkenntnissen*. GA 27.

25. 'Consonant, vowel – nerve, blood' appears here for the first time in English. The German title is *Das Seelenleben in seiner Äusserung in Sprache und Gesang oder in Bewegung und Haltung, Konsonant, Vokal – Nerv, Blut*. It is published in Rudolf Steiner, *Eurythmie die Offenbarung der Sprechenden Seele*, Rudolf Steiner Verlag, Dornach 1972. GA 277.

26. *Cosmosophy*, vol. II, Rudolf Steiner, Completion Press, 1997.

The German title is *Anthroposophie als Kosmosophie. Zweiter Teil: Die Gestaltung des Menschen als Ergebnis kosmischer Wirkungen.* GA 208.

27. 'Light and weight' is an excerpt from a lecture delivered shortly after the Christmas Foundation Meeting, 12 January 1924. The lecture is titled 'Occult Schools in the Eighteenth and first half of the Nineteenth Century'. Rudolf Steiner, *Rosicrucianism and Modern Initiation*, Rudolf Steiner Press, 1965. The German title is *Mysterienstätten des Mittelalters.* GA 233a.

28. *The Healing Process — Spirit, Nature and our Bodies*, Rudolf Steiner, Anthroposophic Press, 2000. This book is a translation of *Anthroposophische Menschenerkenntnis und Medizin*, Rudolf Steiner Verlag, Dornach 1971. GA 319. The selection in this text is from a lecture delivered in The Hague, 16 November 1923.

29. 'Metamorphosis' is an introduction to a performance in Dornach, 12 December 1920. The text is a manuscript in the Rudolf Steiner Library, Ghent, NY.

30. 'Lynceus' is a facsimile of a standard *Auftakt* (introduction) form drawn by Rudolf Steiner. The original is in the Rudolf Steiner Nachlassverwaltung in Dornach. It is published in *Eurythmieformen*, Band III, Rudolf Steiner Verlag, Dornach, 1990, page 177.

31. 'I U A' is a facsimile of a standard form drawn by Rudolf Steiner. The original is in the Rudolf Steiner Nachlassverwaltung in Dornach. It is published in Rudolf Steiner, *Die Entstehung u. Entwickelung der Eurythmie*, Rudolf Steiner Verlag, Dornach 1965. GA 277a.

32. Photo — Chorus from a Greek Drama. Cara Groot, *Marie Savitch Im Leben u. Wirken für Rudolf Steiners Eurythmischen Impuls*, Verlag am Goetheanum, Dornach 1989.

33. 'Costumes and colour' is from Rudolf Steiner, *Eurythmy as Visible Speech*, Anthroposophical Publishing Company, London 1956. The German title is *Eurythmie als sichtbare Sprache*. GA 279.

34. 'Lighting and costume indications' are selections from Rudolf Steiner, *Beleuchtungs u. Kostümangaben – Ton-Eurythmie*, Rudolf Steiner Verlag, 1975. These selections appear here in English for the first time.

35. 'Light eurythmy' is a selection of excerpts from Rudolf Steiner's introductions to eurythmy performances. These appear here in English for the first time. The German source is Rudolf Steiner, *Eurythmie, die Offenbarung der Sprechenden Seele*, Rudolf Steiner Verlag, Dornach 1972. GA 277.

36. The archival photo of Rudolf Steiner with the Goetheanum Stage Group is published in Tatiana Kisseleff, *Eurythmie Arbeit mit Rudolf Steiner*, Verlag die Pforte, Basel 1982.

37. 'The eurythmy training' is an excerpt from a meeting that took place following a pedagogical conference, Friday, 30 March 1923, 9:00 a.m.–2:00 p.m., and is published in Rudolf Steiner, *Faculty Meetings with Rudolf Steiner*, vol. 2, Anthroposophic Press, 1998. The German title is *Konferenzen mit den Lehrern der Freien Waldorfschule in Stuttgart*. GA 300b.

38. 'What the actor learns from eurythmy' is an excerpt of a lecture given in Dornach 15 September 1924. It is published in Rudolf Steiner, *Speech and Drama*, Anthroposophic Press, Spring Valley, New York, and Rudolf Steiner Press, London 1986. The German is entitled *Sprachgestaltung und Dramatische Kunst*. GA 282.

39. 'In the current epoch of the earth' is from Rudolf Steiner, *Correspondence and Documents*, Rudolf Steiner Press, and Anthroposophic Press, 1988. The German title is *Briefwechsel*

und Dokumente 1901–1925: Rudolf Steiner/Marie Steiner-von Sivers. GA 262.

40. 'Introductory Words' is an introduction to a performance given for the International Delegates' Congress of the Anthroposophical Society, 22 July 1923. The lecture is titled 'How Eurhythmy Arises out of Anthroposophy' and was published by the Anthroposophical Society of Great Britain in the news-sheet *Anthroposophical Movement*, vol. V, no. 37, 9 September 1928. The German is published with the title *Die imaginative Offenbarung der Sprache* in Rudolf Steiner, *Eurythmie, die Offenbarung der Sprechenden Seele*, Rudolf Steiner Verlag, 1972. GA 277.

41. The photo of the south view of the First Goetheanum is from *The Life and Work of Rudolf Steiner, From the Turn of the Century to his Death* by Guenther Wachsmuth, Whittier Books, Inc., New York 1955, p. 116. The first edition of this book was titled *Der Geburt der Geisteswissenschaft* ('The Birth of Spiritual Science') *c.* 1941.

42. 'The building and eurythmy are one' is an excerpt from Magdalene Siegloch, *How the New Art of Eurythmy Began*, Temple Lodge Press, 1997, and *Der Goetheanum gedanke*, Rudolf Steiner Nachlassverwaltung, Dornach 1961. GA 36.

43. Photo—First Goetheanum stage is from *Der Baugedanke des Goetheanum* by Rudolf Steiner, Stuttgart 1958, p. 82.

44. 'The stained glass windows' is from *Architecture as a Synthesis of the Arts*, Part II: 'Ways to a New Style of Architecture', Rudolf Steiner Press, London 1999. GA 286.

45. 'Imagination, Inspiration, Intuition' is an introduction to a performance given during the Christmas Foundation Meeting, 23 December 1923. It is published in Rudolf Steiner, *The Christmas Conference*, Anthroposophic Press, 1990. The Ger-

man title is *Die Weihnachtstagung zur Begründung der Allgemeinen Anthroposophischen Gesellschaft*. GA 260.

46. 'Eurythmy is a Moving Sculpture' is an introduction to a performance given during the Christmas Foundation Meeting, 26 December 1923. It is published in Rudolf Steiner, *Eurythmy as Visible Speech*, Anthroposophic Publishing Company, 1956. GA 279. The German is in Rudolf Steiner, *Eurythmie, die Offenbarung der Sprechenden Seele*, Rudolf Steiner Verlag, 1972. GA 277.

47. The eurythmy programme for members is published in Rudolf Steiner, *Eurythmie, die Offenbarung der Sprechenden Seele*, Rudolf Steiner Verlag, 1972. GA 277.

48. 'The Foundation Stone' is an introduction to a performance given in Dornach on 22 April 1924. The German title is *Die Weisheits-Worte der Grundsteinlegung*. It is published in Rudolf Steiner, *Eurythmie, die Offenbarung der Sprechenden Seele*, Rudolf Steiner Verlag, Dornach 1972. GA 277.

49. 'About the Being of eurythmy' is an introduction to a performance given in Berlin on 14 September 1919 and is published in Rudolf Steiner, *Eurythmie, die Offenbarung der Sprechenden Seele*, Rudolf Steiner Verlag, 1972. GA 277. It is published here in English for the first time.

Further reading

By Rudolf Steiner

Eurythmy as Visible Speech, Anthroposophical Publishing Company, London 1955.

Eurythmy as Visible Singing, The Anderida Music Trust, Robinswood Press, Stourbridge 1996.

(and Lory Smits) *Eurythmy: Its Birth and Development*, Anastasi Ltd., Weobley, Herefordshire, 2002.

Curative Eurythmy, Rudolf Steiner Press, London 1983.

A Lecture on Eurythmy, Rudolf Steiner Press, London 1977.

An Introduction to Eurythmy, Anthroposophic Press, Spring Valley, NY, 1984.

The Inner Nature of Music, Anthroposophic Press, Spring Valley, NY, 1983.

Twelve Moods, Mercury Press, Spring Valley, NY, 1984.

The Arts and their Mission, The Anthroposophic Press, Spring Valley, NY, 1964.

Art in the Light of Mystery Wisdom, Anthroposophic Press, New York City, Harry Collison, London 1935.

Art as Seen in the Light of Mystery Wisdom, Rudolf Steiner Press, London 1984.

Art as Spiritual Activity, Anthroposophic Press, Hudson, NY, 1998.

The Nature and Origin of the Arts, Mercury Press, Spring Valley, NY, 1992.

Creative Speech, Rudolf Steiner Press, London 1978.

Speech and Drama, Anthroposophic Press, Spring Valley, NY, Rudolf Steiner Press, London 1986.

Poetry and the Art of Speech, London School of Speech Formation, Rudolf Steiner Press, London 1981.

Other authors

Francine Adams, *Eurythmy for the Elementary Grades*, AWSNA, 1997.

Werner Barfod, *IAO and the Eurythmy Meditations*, Mercury Press, Spring Valley, NY, 2001.

Elizabeth Baumann, *Eurythmy Therapy in Practice and Other Essays*, St Christophe, Fechy (Vaud).

Michael Brater et al., *Eurythmy in the Workplace*, Rudolf Steiner Books, Chicago 1988.

Reg Down, *Leaving Room for the Angels*, AWSNA, Fair Oaks, CA, revised edition, 2004.

Annemarie Dubach, *Eurythmy – Recollections*, Eurythmy Spring Valley, Chestnut Ridge, NY, 2000.

Annemarie Dubach-Donath, *Basic Principles of Eurythmy*, Rudolf Steiner Publishing Co., London/Anthroposophic Press 1937.

Maria Glass, *Experience in Remedial Eurythmy*, Care for Eurythmy, Forest Row, East Sussex, 2004.

Margarete Kirchner-Bockholt, MD, *Fundamental Principles of Curative Eurythmy*, Rudolf Steiner Press, London 1977.

Thomas Poplawski, *Eurythmy – Rhythm, Dance & Soul*, Floris Books, Anthroposophic Press, Hudson, NY, 1998.

Marjorie Raffé, Cecil Harwood, Marguerite Lundgren, *Eurythmy and the Impulse of Dance*, Rudolf Steiner Press, London 1974.

Marie Savitch, *Marie Steiner-von Sivers*, Rudolf Steiner Press, London 1967.

Magdalene Siegloch, *How the New Art of Eurythmy Began*, Temple Lodge Press, London 1997.

Marjorie Spock, *Eurythmy*, Anthroposophic Press, Spring Valley, NY, 1980.

Lea van der Pals, *The Human Being as Music*, Robinswood Press, Stourbridge 1981.

Mollie von Heider, *Come Unto These Yellow Sands*, Rudolf Steiner College Press, Fair Oaks, CA, 1998.

Mollie von Heider, *And Then Take Hands*, Celestial Arts, Millbrae, CA, 1981.

Elena Zuccoli, *From the Tone Eurythmy Work*, Walter Keller Press, Dornach, Switzerland, 1981.

Photo credits

Contacts

Section for the Arts of Eurythmy, Speech, Drama and Music
Goetheanum
Ruttiweg 45
CH-4143 Dornach 1
Switzerland
Tel: +41 (0)61 706 42 42
Fax: +41 (0)61 706 43 14
Email: sekretariat@goetheanum.ch
Web: www.goetheanum.ch

(For trainings follow the link to 'Eurythmie Ausbildungen'.)

About the Editor

Beth Usher is a eurythmist with a eurythmy therapy practice in Austin, Texas. She met anthroposophy as a teenager through Professor Emeritus Ernst Katz while completing a Bachelor's degree at University of Michigan in Ann Arbor. Graduation from the eurythmy training in Spring Valley (New York) in 1983 was followed by teaching in the School of Eurythmy (Spring Valley), in the New York School for the Deaf, and in the Northern Lights School in Wilmington (New York). She and her husband currently lecture, teach and perform at anthroposophic conferences in the United States, particularly with initiatives for young people.

Note Regarding Rudolf Steiner's Lectures

The lectures and addresses contained in this volume have been translated from the German, which is based on stenographic and other recorded texts that were in most cases never seen or revised by the lecturer. Hence, due to human errors in hearing and transcription, they may contain mistakes and faulty passages. Every effort has been made to ensure that this is not the case. Some of the lectures were given to audiences more familiar with anthroposophy; these are the so-called 'private' or 'members' lectures. Other lectures, like the written works, were intended for the general public. The difference between these, as Rudolf Steiner indicates in his *Autobiography*, is twofold. On the one hand, the members' lectures take for granted a background in and commitment to anthroposophy; in the public lectures this was not the case. At the same time, the members' lectures address the concerns and dilemmas of the members, while the public work speaks directly out of Steiner's own understanding of universal needs. Nevertheless, as Rudolf Steiner stresses: 'Nothing was ever said that was not solely the result of my direct experience of the growing content of anthroposophy. There was never any question of concessions to the prejudices and preferences of the members. Whoever reads these privately printed lectures can take them to represent anthroposophy in the fullest sense. Thus it was possible without hesitation — when the complaints in this direction became too persistent — to depart from the custom of circulating this material "For members only". But it must be borne in mind that faulty passages do occur in these reports not revised by myself.' Earlier in the same chapter, he states: 'Had I been able to correct them [the private lectures], the restriction *for members only* would have been unnecessary from the beginning.'

The original German editions on which this text is based were published by Rudolf Steiner Verlag, Dornach, Switzerland in the collected edition (*Gesamtausgabe*, 'GA') of Rudolf Steiner's work. All publications are edited by the Rudolf Steiner Nachlassverwaltung (estate), which wholly owns both Rudolf Steiner Verlag and the Rudolf Steiner Archive. The organization relies solely on donations to continue its activity.

For further information please contact:

Rudolf Steiner Archiv
Postfach 135
CH-4143 Dornach

or:

www.rudolf-steiner.com